GERONTOLOGICAL SOCIAL WORK

Ilene L. Nathanson, DSW, is Director of Social Work Programs and Associate Professor of Health Care and Public Administration at the C.W. Post Campus, Long Island University, where she also serves as Director of the Center on Aging. Dr. Nathanson's research and professional activities have largely focused on developing and applying the concepts of professional and interdisciplinary role relationships in gerontological service provision. Her research has resulted in the establishment of Earnest Affiliates for Retired Persons (EARP), the first comprehensive service center for older adults in the community—representing the collaborative contributions of a range of disciplines, including law, medicine, social work, psychology, nursing, finance, and geriatric care management.

Terry Tirrito, DSW, is an associate professor of social work at the University of South Carolina in Columbia, South Carolina. Previously she has worked as a gerontologist in private practice, as a nursing home consultant, and as director of social services in a long-term-care facility. Dr. Tirrito is a graduate of Fordham University in New York with a degree in gerontological social work. She is an international teacher and researcher and has lectured and taught in Korea, Hong Kong, Toronto, Israel, England, Scotland, and France. She and Dr. Nathanson are coauthors of *Elder Practice: A Multidisciplinary Approach to Working with Older Adults in the Community* (1996).

GERONTOLOGICAL SOCIAL WORK

Theory into Practice

Ilene L. Nathanson, DSW, BCD
Terry T. Tirrito, DSW

Springer Publishing Company

Springer Publishing Company, Inc.
536 Broadway
New York, NY 10012-3955

Cover design by Margaret Dunin
Acquisitions Editor: Bill Tucker
Production Editor: Susan Gamer

00 01/ 5 4 3 2

Library of Congress Cataloging-in-Publication Data
Nathanson, Ilene.
    Gerontological social work: theory into practice / Ilene L. Nathanson,
Terry T. Tirrito.
        p.   cm.
    Includes bibliographical references and index.
    ISBN 0-8261-9890-2
    1. Social work with the aged—United States. 2. Gerontology—United
States.
    I. Tirrito, Terry. 1945–   . II Title.
HV1461.N324   1997   97-23144
362.6—dc21   CIP

Printed in the United States of America

For my grandfather, William Nathanson, who above all wanted me to become a writer. For my teachers at the Wurzweiler School of Social Work, who provided the inspiration for this writing, and especially for Professor Emeritus Everett Wilson—who had the good fortune of knowing and learning from Ruth Smalley. For the building of new frameworks on classical foundations.

—I.L.N.

This book is dedicated to my daughter, Cathy, my son, Sal, and to Michael Cosmo, whose aging I expect will be very different, and to my mother-in-law Catherine who taught me about aging with dignity.

—T.T.T.

Contents

Preface

There are many fine works on social work practice. Similarly, there are a number of fine books that focus on the special needs of older adults and the various individual and treatment methodologies that seem to be effective with this age group. There is, however, no single work in the literature that presents a comprehensive approach to counseling the elderly within an integrated theoretical framework. This book is designed to provide such a resource.

There is a long-standing debate in social work between those who view the profession as being defined by its generic underpinnings and those who have argued for a more categorical concept, emphasizing the distinctive elements of practice in the various fields, such as mental health, health care, and child welfare.

Gerontological social work cuts across both of these positions, since older individuals are served in all arenas of practice — from group services, such as senior centers, to psychiatric services. The only common denominator among those who call themselves gerontological social workers is the age of their clients.

Therefore, a new concept of social work practice is required to integrate these two positions — if one is to understand gerontological social work as being uniquely specialized. Moreover, clear connections with social work theory must be elaborated in order to demonstrate that this new concept is rooted in social work ideology.

This book defines the principles that undergird the social work profession. It goes on to define the special needs of older people and the different social situations in which these needs are expressed, such as marriage, the extended family, social welfare, the legal and political system, and the health care system. We define the role of gerontological social workers in each of these arenas, and various specialized practice technologies that have been developed for use in each of these arenas. Some encounters with clients call for traditional approaches. For example, the social worker who is assigned to hear concerns of residents in a home for adults and the hospital social worker who is helping to facilitate a client's discharge back to the community have to understand the scope and limits of their responsibilities within a generic professional framework. Yet both of these social workers will have to modulate their practice techniques to suit the special needs of the older clients they serve. What is the tie between standard practice and "gerontological" social work? Our book addresses this question.

The book is organized as follows. It begins with a delineation of the concepts inherent in social work and specifically in gerontological social work. We address the historical contrast between the functionalists, or task-centered social work practitioners, and the psychoanalytically oriented practitioners. An integrative concept is presented to connect the two approaches. The different arenas of work with clients are then discussed. Common problems in various fields of service delivery are defined. Case vignettes are used to illustrate situations commonly encountered in social work. In these cases, relevant background material is included, as well as follow-up questions to stimulate class discussion. The book provides a medium for the development of alternative strategies for intervention and the assessment of these strategies. Special emphasis is placed on sharpening communication skills; the cases also include verbal exchanges which illustrate the use of different skills, such as the ability to listen, "partialize," and paraphrase or restate feeling or content. Finally, we identify the legal and political implications of gerontological social work in the various arenas. Although social work is primarily a client-centered profession, it is differentiated from other mental health professions (e.g., psychology and psychiatry) by its emphatic concern with the institutional context in which it is practiced.

Social work ideology offers an excellent framework for the provision of comprehensive services to an aging population. The social needs of older people clearly are as central to their functioning as mental health or health concerns. As individuals age, their dependence on the strength of formal and informal supports increases. This book is as much a testament to the significance of social work, and its theoretical underpinnings, as to the significance of the older person's place in our society. As the population ages, the profession has a chance to renew itself, in its contribution to the successful reconciliation of people's changing needs and the purposes of the institutions designed to serve these needs.

Introduction

S ocial work is a dynamic profession. It changes with the changing requirements of society. Its history reflects these changes and will be revisited in chapter 1 of this book. However, there are fundamental principles that guide the growth of this profession. These have remained unaltered despite shifting social needs and advancing technologies. Fields of practice may change and methodologies may evolve, but the beliefs and values that guide these changes are what make up the profession of social work.

This book is dedicated to the fundamental purpose of social work as expressed by Ruth Smalley. In the first line of the first chapter of her *Theory for Social Work Practice* (1967) she states: "The underlying purpose of all social work effort is to release human power in individuals for personal fulfillment and social good, and to release social power for the creation of the kinds of society, social institutions, and social policy which make self-realization most possible for all men" (p. 1). This statement (to which we would, of course, now add "and women") captures the essential synthesis of two driving forces behind social work practice: the common bond between individual interest and the social good. This statement is what provides coherence and integrity to the self-actualizing profession that is social work.

In this book, we do not add anything new to the fundamentals of social work practice. We simply demonstrate the application of these fundamentals to a specific field of practice, that of services for the aging. Growth in services to older people has resulted in a need for professionals in all fields of human service to redefine their roles and activities vis-à-vis their clients (patients) and other professionals (Tirrito, Nathanson, & Langer, 1996). Social work practice with older persons, or gerontological social work, cuts across many traditional fields of practice and all three primary methodologies: casework, group work, and community organization. In addition, psychiatric social work with older persons calls for some variations in the application of concepts derived from the body of psychoanalytic theory. We outline the application of principles for general social work practice to social work practice with the aging in specific arenas. We combine general principles and specific knowledge and technologies in demonstrating the unique arrangement of these factors in work with older people in various social contexts.

The need for an examination of the principles that guide social work practice with older persons is obvious. Thirty-one million people over age 65 and 3 million over age 85 currently require the attention of professionals in the various disciplines, including social work. The over-85 group is the one growing most rapidly, having increased by 300% since 1960 (Ginsberg, 1992). Older people are among the most physically frail and socially, financially, and legally most vulnerable members of American society. The growing importance of older persons to human service institutions cannot be overstated, given the high risk status of this group for diseases such as Alzheimer's and the associated social and financial demands of long term care. On the brighter side, health professionals must also address the changing recreational, educational, and employment requirements of an expanding cohort of healthy, older, productive members of society. This book is designed as a guide for social workers in different organizational settings and practice arenas to promote more effective work with older age cohorts.

Chapter 1 defines the theoretical framework of the book. Concepts inherent in general social work practice are integrated into a model of gerontological social work. The concepts are drawn primarily from the work of Ruth Smalley but are enriched by the elaboration of specific techniques that we have used in our work with older people.

Chapter 2 presents the practice theory in the form of a process model and operationalizes the concepts presented in Chapter 1. In succeeding chapters, we will selectively illustrate the application of these concepts in specific fields of practice.

Chapter 3 provides an overview of the special needs of older people in the various social contexts, including the family, informal and formal social services, health and legal services, religious and business communities, and the larger political context. This knowledge is necessary in order for the gerontological social worker to properly "tune in" to the needs of older clients.

Chapter 4 examines the role of the social worker in providing mental health assistance to older individuals and their families. A distinction is drawn between agency and private practice arrangements, and generic—that is, general—principles of practice are applied to case examples in both settings. The particular emphasis in Chapter 4 is on illustrating the meaning of diagnosis and contract in the proposed theory of practice.

Chapter 5 describes the role of the social worker in the provision of formal social services. The case example in this chapter illustrates the application of an integrative model of gerontological social work practice to a case of an older applicant for Meals-on-Wheels. The case is designed specifically to highlight the significance of comprehensive biopsychosocial assessment and collaboration in working with older adults. Particular emphasis is placed on the impact of culture on assessment and work with the client.

Chapter 6 describes the role of the social worker in geriatric health care. Three settings are discussed: hospital, nursing home, and home care agency. The situations are used to illustrate the principles of assessment and coordination of services.

Chapter 7 explores the role of the social worker in the field of "elder law." The case highlights the mediating function of the social worker in the context of family conflicts. This chapter also explores the implications for policy and planning activities in the legal arena.

Chapter 8 investigates the role of the social worker in regard to the religious and spiritual needs of clients and the purposes of religious institutions. The roles of the social worker as mediator and advocate are addressed.

Chapter 9 addresses institutional obstacles to older people's employment and individual problems that result from typical losses associated with old age, such as death of a spouse. The application of micro and macro methods is explored.

Chapter 10 highlights the role of the social worker in the political environment and explores the planning function of a group worker in a community center who is assigned to an older adults' social group. The group is interested in redefining its purpose and becoming more involved in social reform activities.

Chapter 11 focuses on communication issues in gerontological social work practice. Since relationships develop through communication and relationship is viewed within this framework as the social work method, then it is incumbent on gerontological social work practitioners to understand effective means of communicating with older adults.

Chapter 12, the final chapter, offers a summary of the principles of the integrative gerontological social work practice methodology presented in the book. The chapter addresses the implications of the methodology for research, education, and social policy.

REFERENCES

Ginsberg, L. (1992). *Social work almanac.* Washington, DC: National Association of Social Workers (NASW).

Smalley, R. (1967). *Theory for social work practice.* New York: Columbia University Press.

Tirrito, T., Nathanson, I., & Langer, N. (1996). *Elder practice: A multidisciplinary approach to working with older people in the community.* Columbia, SC: The University of South Carolina Press.

CHAPTER 1

Social Work Practice Revisited

INTRODUCTION

Gerontological social work is being defined as a specialized area of social work with older people which cuts across all fields and methodologies. It is unique in its formulation of specialization insofar as social work specializations are typically defined in terms of (1) field of practice or (2) particular methodology, such as casework, group work, or community organization.

In this chapter we develop a conceptual framework for gerontological social work that draws on traditional principles of professional practice. The concepts are combined within a framework that is integrative in its orientation; in other words, it provides a generic methodological direction to this crosscutting specialization. We offer a guide to practice with older people in all fields of service delivery. In subsequent chapters—in recognition of the specific expertise that informs practice in the various fields—we identify comparative differences in the nature of the work in these varying service contexts.

The present chapter begins with the roots of social work practice and a review of the contrasting approaches represented by functionalism and the psychoanalytic or diagnostic approach. It then develops an integrated practice methodology that will be applied throughout the book to the various fields of delivery of services to the aging.

1

HISTORICAL BACKGROUND

Social work is a profession whose development expresses the fundamental law of dialectics. This is the understanding that there is a reciprocal and dynamic relationship between ideas and actions in a constantly evolving institutional framework. As the need for new answers to social problems has continued to emerge, social work continues to struggle with the challenge of identifying the balance between the stable and the temporal in our definition of professional mission and methodology.

We began as a profession that was dedicated to the alleviation of social ills. The early preoccupation with causes did not transfer into an equal concern with methods until the early part of the twentieth century, when two different schools of thought evolved on the nature of social problems and the appropriate method for coping with the ills of individuals in society. These two schools of thought are known as the functional and the diagnostic, or psychoanalytic.

The early social caseworkers embraced the psychological insights of Sigmund Freud in formulating a method for treatment of individuals and families. These pioneering efforts are exemplified by the contributions of such writers as Virginia Robinson, and subsequently Gordon Hamilton, Charlotte Towle, and Florence Hollis. They were concerned primarily with the individual—in contrast to earlier social workers, who were more focused on the alleviation of social ills and promoting social purposes through programs (Smalley, 1967).

Functional social work, which developed at the University of Pennsylvania under the leadership of Virginia Robinson and Jesse Taft, provided a contrast to the diagnostic approach (as it would become known) formulated by Hamilton, Towle and Hollis. The functional approach differed from the diagnostic approach in its emphasis on the client's health rather than on pathology, and on the centrality of the client to the definition of his or her own purpose. Most important, functionalism theoretically links the client's "growth purpose" to the provision of a service within an agency framework. Growth or movement for clients is inexorably connected to their ability to avail themselves of, or perhaps even alter, the service that is being provided. In other words, if clients succeed in achieving the purpose they set for themselves (within the context of the services provided by the agency), then they are considered to have "moved" or "grown" insofar as they have achieved this particular purpose. Change is measured in terms of achievement of purpose or promotion of "function." This theoretical linkage squarely placed concern for a program on the same primary level as concern for the individual. We elaborate on this and other principles of functional social work later in this chapter (Brill, 1990; Haynes & Holmes, 1994; Robinson, 1950).

The 1960s witnessed the "War on Poverty" and a shift in social work professionals' concerns away from method and toward the implementation of social programs aimed at alleviating social disadvantages. As Ruth Smalley (1967) points out, the reduced concern with method in the social work literature of the 1960s appeared to reflect a lack of appreciation for the link between method and a promotion of the social task.

Although alleviating social ills has remained a focus of the social work literature through the 1980s and into the 1990s, interest in practice methodology has clearly been reinstated as a priority. However, developments in psychosocial treatment methods, advances in biopsychiatric remedies, administrative technologies, advocacy methodologies, and changing and increasingly diverse social needs require social workers to continually reassess goals, objectives, and modes of intervention for individuals and social groups. In this book we investigate the needs of a particular social constituency — the aging. We also evaluate the generic underpinnings of practice in this area of service delivery and the application of specialized technologies in the various fields of gerontological practice.

What do we take as gospel in the formulation of our goals and the assessment of appropriate technologies? We believe that the functionalist orientation provides a generic framework for the development of a specialized methodology in gerontological social work. In other words, functional social work is the frame on which we can construct a guide to the various roles and functions of gerontological social workers. We return to Smalley's *Theory for Social Work Practice* (1967) for a generic concept and address its application to gerontological social work.

GENERIC PRINCIPLES OF SOCIAL WORK PRACTICE

PRINCIPLE I

> That diagnosis, or understanding of the phenomenon served, is most effective for all the social work processes which is related to the use of the service; which is developed, in part, in the course of giving the service, with the engagement and participation of the clientele served; which is recognized as being subject to continuous modification as the phenomenon changes; and which is put out by the worker for the clientele to use, as appropriate in the course of the service. (p. 134)

With this first statement of principle, Smalley (1967) cautions against the attempt to understand "the total person in his total situation." Diagnosis is used by Smalley as the process by which the worker helps the clients (individuals, groups or communities) to define their own goals for themselves as these goals fall within or coincide with the goals of the specific program being administered. Diagnosis or understanding of the client's need for the service is not static but develops in the course of a relationship through which the worker helps the individual or group utilize or modify the service being provided. This concept contrasts with the psychoanalytic concept which views the diagnosis as deriving strictly from the worker's assessment of the client. Study and diagnosis then inform the treatment plan, which is decided by the worker for the client. In the functional formulation, the worker diagnoses the client's need for the service, the client's ability to use the service, and the method by which the service is achieved—not the client's pathology and what needs to be changed. Method is a relationship process defined by principles of action aimed at a defined social purpose. The social worker does not exist outside the growth process as the analytic expert but rather is a partner in a mutual activity. The reiterative and reciprocal nature of the association between diagnosis and relationship is illustrated in Figure 1.1.

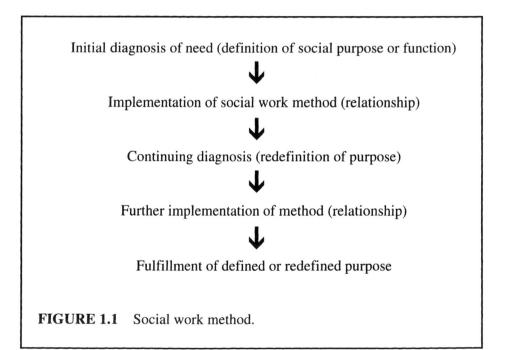

Initial diagnosis of need (definition of social purpose or function)

↓

Implementation of social work method (relationship)

↓

Continuing diagnosis (redefinition of purpose)

↓

Further implementation of method (relationship)

↓

Fulfillment of defined or redefined purpose

FIGURE 1.1   Social work method.

This emphasis on relationship and specificity of purpose is reiterated in Smalley's third and fifth principles. Most older people seek assistance for a specific problem from a specific type of agency. This formulation provides for the specificity of focus that is required for the delivery of the particular service which takes place in the context of a human relationship.

PRINCIPLE II

> The effectiveness of any social work process, primary or secondary, is furthered by the worker's conscious, knowing use of time phases in the process (beginnings, middles, and endings) in order that the particular potential in each time phase may be fully exploited for the other's use. (p. 142)

Principle II supports the relevance of the specificity of the time frame to the delivery of the human service in either an individual or a group format. It is a principle that is well understood in administrative process, a secondary social work process. Its relevance to the primary methods of casework and group work is identified by Smalley. In application to work with the aging, the use of time is clearly relevant because older people do not have a lifetime ahead of them for self-discovery. The energy of the worker and the client is directed by the specificity of time as well as function which facilitates the achievement of desired outcomes.

PRINCIPLE III

> The use of agency function and function in professional role gives focus, content, and direction to social work processes, assures accountability to society and to agency, and provides the partialization, the concreteness, the "difference," the "given" which further productive engagement. (p. 151)

The helping relationship takes place within the context of an agency. Not only is the client strengthened by the direction given to the work by time and focus; so too the worker is strengthened in promoting the connection between the needs of those he or she serves and the purpose of the agency. As a gerontological social worker, if all I am responsible for serving is the population for whom my agency makes a particular service available, I can direct my energy to the interest of serving a particular need of a particular group and I am strengthened.

PRINCIPLE IV

> A conscious, knowing use of structure as it evolves from and is related to function and process introduces "form," which furthers the effectiveness of all the social work processes, both primary and secondary. (p. 162)

Smalley uses the term form to denote structure of any kind—time, place, policy, agency, function, relationship. In this statement, Smalley underscores the importance of efficiency and organizational design to the provision of service. She is addressing the administrative and planning expertise that is crucial to the efficient delivery of a particular service. In casework or group work, this expertise may have to do with the processes of contract, role definition and differentiation, and case or group planning (including scheduling of tasks or activities). In community organizing efforts, this type of expertise may have to do with program development, system coordination, or perhaps strategic planning activities. Principle IV relates to all fields of social work practice, nonetheless.

PRINCIPLE V

> All social work processes, to be effective as processes in social work, require the use of relationship to engage the other in making and acting on choices or decisions as the core of working toward the accomplishment of a purpose identified as own purpose, within the purpose of the service being offered (p. 167).

In Principle V, Smalley further identifies the centrality of the relationship between worker and client to performance or accomplishment of the task. In the functional framework, method is defined as a relationship process. We will elaborate on the concept of relationship in chapter 3. Simply put, relationship is a connection or alliance between or among people and develops by means of communication or interaction. This connection is viewed as crucial to the effectiveness of all social work actions.

In addition, the individual's purpose and that of the service organization must be one. This places a great deal of responsibility on the worker to identify what is in the best interest of the client and also to ensure that the agency serves that interest. Not only is growth of the client rooted in the purpose of the agency, but the health of the organization is rooted in the growth of its clients. This concept of mutuality is further elaborated by Schwartz and Zalba (1971). The worker is viewed as a mediator in the exchange between the client and the client system in promoting the fulfillment of a purpose mutually agreed on.

This principle of helping clients to help themselves within the limits of agency function once again is relevant to all fields of practice, including the various fields of services for the aging. Principle V, like Principles I to IV, is based on a view of human beings as growth-affirming and on the importance of structure to this growth process.

These five principles describe our own orientation in our formulation of a social work practice methodology. They represent the generic aspects of the formulation. We endorse the principles pertaining to the power of specific purpose and use of time in facilitating the process, the use of relationship in promoting understanding and movement in the process, and the importance of structure to the realization of individual and social goals. We will demonstrate the applicability of these concepts to practice with the aged in a variety of service settings. We will discuss their applicability to the different modalities of practice (e.g., casework, group work, and community organization). What we add to this formulation is knowledge about the specific individual and group needs of older people, including psychological and biological insights that inform a professional diagnosis or understanding of these needs. Our integrative methodology basically represents the combining of the generic principles outlined above with specific knowledge of older people essential to the understanding of social work practice in the various fields of aging services. There is one generic principle of gerontological social work, however, that we would add to Smalley's theory, and that is the following.

PRINCIPLE VI

In order to be effective in promoting principles I through V with older clients, the worker's understanding of clients' needs must include knowledge of their need for service not only from the agency providing the service but from all the agencies and organizations within the "client system."

Principle VI has been added to demonstrate the necessity of comprehensive assessment and collaborative effort to the provision of service to an older population. We believe that despite specific variations in social work knowledge and practice in the different fields of service delivery, all gerontological social workers must be able to formulate a comprehensive assessment of their clients' needs for a range of health, social, legal, and religious or spiritual services and must be able to coordinate referrals and conduct follow-up evaluations. Collaboration is part of the social work function with older people. To be effective, the social worker must be able to engage not only the client but also the client system.

Gerontological social work practice is the integration of generalist principles of practice with specialized knowledge of issues of aging and knowledge of specific settings of practice.

FIGURE 1.2   Integrative gerontological social work.

At first glance it may appear that Principle VI contradicts Principle I. Principle I calls for specificity of purpose. Principle VI calls for comprehensive assessment. We believe, however, that this apparent difference can be reconciled. *Diagnosis* is used in Principle I to mean diagnosis of a client's need for, and ability to use, a specific service. But, the client may have other needs for services which go beyond the scope of the specific social work function. It is incumbent on the social worker to identify these needs and make appropriate referrals for additional assistance. Thus, the social worker can provide a general assessment and still be guided by a specific purpose.

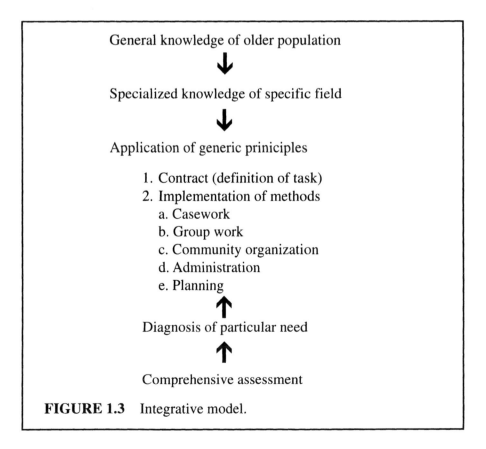

General knowledge of older population

Specialized knowledge of specific field

Application of generic priniciples

1. Contract (definition of task)
2. Implementation of methods
   a. Casework
   b. Group work
   c. Community organization
   d. Administration
   e. Planning

Diagnosis of particular need

Comprehensive assessment

FIGURE 1.3   Integrative model.

These six principles are the foundation of our generic paradigm. In chapter 2, we present a process model that represents the application of the above principles. It is the juxtaposition of these generic principles and the specific knowledge of the needs of older people in relation to various aspects of social reality that provide the foundation for our integrative methodology (Figures 1.2 and 1.3 opposite).

The integrative model calls for the worker to have comprehensive understanding of an older population and specialized knowledge of a particular field of interaction (e.g., legal or medical). Application of the model requires that the worker have expertise in different modalities of professional practice (e.g., casework and group work) and be able to select the preferred modality in a particular situation. The worker must identify organizational and institutional goals as well as individual or group goals, since individual growth is linked to institutional growth.

In chapter 2, we delineate the application of the generic principles in the different phases of work to further elaborate the proposed integrative model.

REFERENCES

Brill, N. (1990). *Working with people: The helping process* (4th Ed.). New York: Longman.

Haynes, K.S., & Holmes, K.A. (1994). *Invitation to social work.* New York: Longman.

Robinson, V. (1950). *Dynamics of supervision under functional controls.* Philadelphia: University of Pennsylvania Press.

Schwartz, W., & Zalba, S. (1971). *The practice of group work.* New York: Columbia University Press.

Smalley, R. (1967). *Theory for social work practice.* New York: Columbia University Press.

CHAPTER 2

Integrative Model of
Gerontological Social Work

In this chapter we further elaborate our theory of practice. Here we outline the variables involved in the different phases of work and identify the application of the practice principles in each phase.

In chapter 1, we outlined Smalley's generic principles of practice, which reflect a certain understanding of the interplay between individual growth and institutional growth. Although the functionalists were the first to define the forces that link individual growth with organizational or institutional development, this perspective has been maintained in the social work literature through the writings of Schwartz and Zalba (1971) and, currently, Shulman (1992). Schwartz's interactional model, which is elaborated by Shulman in *The Skills of Helping,* is predicated on a basic assumption of symbiosis, or the mutual need of individuals and the systems that matter to them. This assumption grows out of a functional framework as presented by Smalley. Shulman describes a possible pitfall of viewing the social worker as a mediator between the needs of clients and the purposes of service agencies. It may lead social workers to view their role as limited to the purposes set out for them in agency policy. The interactional model stresses the need for the worker to be an advocate, if necessary, for the client's interest, but still emphasizes the importance of clear role definition and establishment of a common ground for clients' needs and agencies' purposes. This assumption of mutuality is a cornerstone of our integrative practice theory and owes its roots to Schwartz and Shulman.

Shown in Figure 2.1 is a process model which identifies the application of the different principles in the different phases of work.

1. General assessment (tuning-in phase)

Age	Gender
Race	Income level
Ethnicity	Education

General assessment also includes an assessment of religious and cultural values. This understanding is critical to respecting differences among perceptions and objectives of clients.

2. Specific biopsychosocial assessment (entry phase)

Assessment of scope of individual or group needs for service
Application of principle I and principle VI

3. Contract (entry phase)

Specific identification of purpose of social work interaction
Application of principle II and principle III

Contract represents an agreement between the client and the worker regarding the goals for the work and the ways of working. The contract is guided by the agency purpose.

4. Implementation phase

Application of principles IV and V
Primary strategies   Secondary strategies
(Direct service)

Casework activities	Administration
Group work activities	Social advocacy
Community organizing	Policy and planning

5. Termination phase

Application of principle II

FIGURE 2.1   Process model.

General assessment or tuning-in is the first phase of work with any client or client group. The worker draws on a general base of knowledge representing scientific understanding of the influence of economic, social, and cultural factors on an individual's or a cultural group's experience and life perspective. This process is the same regardless of the age of the client population and is not unique to the practice of gerontological social work.

Specific biopsychosocial assessment represents an application of two of our stated principles. The work is guided by a specific diagnosis or understanding of the client's need for service and also by a comprehensive understanding of the client's needs. The specific understanding provides a focus for the interaction between worker and client or client group. The broader understanding serves to guide collaborative or multidisciplinary interaction. Collaboration is essential in working with older people because of the complexity of their needs.

Contract provides structure and focus to the work. It is within this structure that a relationship develops between the worker and the client. This relationship is key to movement for the client. Movement is measured in terms of completion of goals as identified in the contract.

Implementation is the next phase. Ruth Smalley distinguishes between primary and secondary methods or modalities of social work. *Primary* is used in the current model to describe direct service activities. *Secondary* methods apply to administrative and planning functions. These secondary processes are viewed as no less important than the primary processes. In fact, in this formulation, individual growth is linked to organizational and institutional developments, since each reflects the engagement and influence of the other. The client is viewed as part of a system or network of interaction in which the health of the system is measured in terms of the health of its constituents. The implementation of both direct and administrative (as well as policy) objectives is best achieved when the worker consciously addresses himself or herself to macro as well as micro and organizational issues. Workers use their relationship with the client or client group, as well as their relationship with members of the larger system of the client's interactions (e.g., agency, family, and other organizations) to promote the interests of the specific client, as well as those of the client's representative group. In the case of gerontological social work, the representative group is defined by the age cohort of the clients and the particular service. (One example of a representative group is the entire group of hospitalized stroke patients over age 60. Another example is the population of older recipients of food stamps in a local department of social services.) In addition, the worker is most effective when following a clear plan with specific objectives and restrictions. These principles suggest that the worker must be an effective administrator in order to achieve positive results.

Termination is the final phase. Here again, specificity of time as well as purpose is important. The worker and clients must complete the job. This formulation assumes that a time frame is effective in harnessing the energies of the worker and clients and facilitating completion of goals. Two specific activities in the termination phase are the identification of major learning and the identification of areas for future work. Some of the learning has to do with how the client has dealt with his or her relationship with the worker. By consolidating an understanding of the relationship, the client may be better prepared to deal with similar interactions in the future. Some of the learning has to do with how the client has learned to handle or manage a life task (Shulman, 1992).

In the chapters that follow, we illustrate the application of these principles in various contexts. Every worker in every setting is expected to perform administrative and planning activities in addition to direct service activities. We recognize, however, that some agency purposes lend themselves more to macro level work than others. A social worker in a group services agency is more likely than a medical social worker to perform community organizing functions: for example, facilitate a neighborhood watch; negotiate changes in bus schedules with the local transit authority to better accommodate the needs of older riders; work with a tenants' association to improve living conditions in an inner-city area; and so on. The broader an agency's function, the broader the scope of the worker's concern (since the purpose of the work derives from that function). However, the functional perspective assigns administrative and planning responsibility to all social workers regardless of their assigned role or their principal target of activity—case, group, or community. Our case examples highlight the application of particular principles of practice, although we support the view that the best social work incorporates micro (individual and small group) activities as well as macro (large group) activities,

Because all workers in all settings need to make a preliminary general assessment of their clients' need for service, Chapter 3 gives an overview of the specialized needs of an older population.

REFERENCES

Schwartz, W., & Zalba, S. (Eds.) (1971). *The practice of group work.* New York: Columbia University Press.

Shulman, L. (1992) *The skills of helping.* Itasca, IL: Peacock Publishers.

CHAPTER 3

Special Needs of Older People: An Overview

The special needs of older people distinguish gerontological social work from other types of practice. Since the work that the social worker performs with clients is a function of the clients' needs, we begin our analysis of the social worker's role in gerontological settings with a delineation of these needs. (Variations in organizational settings further distinguish the work of gerontological social workers; but we will address these other distinctions in later chapters.)

FAMILY, FRIENDSHIP, AND MENTAL HEALTH

No one ever outgrows the need for the support of family and friends. The need for informal help with activities of daily living is certain to grow as one ages. The losses associated with aging often mean that a surviving individual is deprived of the support of his or her spouse just when that support is most necessary. However, contrary to popular belief, children do not abandon their parents, and the rate of nursing home admission is still holding at about 5% of the over-65 age group. Most people in nursing homes are the frailest and oldest of the older population. Up to 25% of nursing home placements are precipitated by the caregiver's illness or death (Hooyman & Kyack, 1993).

With the current surge in the growth of the over-85 age cohort, there is adequate reason to believe that there will be a corresponding surge in the need for both informal and formal services for older people. The risk to the older person grows out of his or her increased physical and sometimes mental vulnerability. Also, although it is pleasant to believe that children will always be there for their parents, no matter how involved they are with work and personal responsibilities—and no matter how great the stresses become—reports indicate that the burdens on informal caregivers are already expanding beyond manageable proportions. This is related to the fact that more women are participating in the job market than in recent decades (Tirrito & Nathanson, 1994): For example, daughters are likely to provide care when a spouse is not capable or available (Kivett, in Hendricks & Hendricks, 1986).

This situation carries a risk of elder neglect and abuse. There are many forms of elder abuse, ranging from financial to physical and even sexual. The older individual may be victimized by a child who is emotionally or financially dependent (Hendricks & Hendricks, 1986). Other, more subtle forms of neglect may stem from a caregiver's inability to reconcile competing demands of spouse, grown children, and work.

The individual's need to bond with family and friends doesn't diminish with age. Nor does the need for physical expression of warmth and caring wane with advancing years. However, for many older people opportunities for closeness and nurturance may not be as readily available as when their grandchildren were young, their spouses and friends were alive, and they didn't rely on anyone to help with the cleaning or shopping. Although most people remain self-reliant for most of their lives, there is likely to come a time when an older person will need some assistance with some aspect of physical or social functioning. Fear of dependency ranks high among threats to older people's sense of personal security (Atchley, 1991). Families often need help coming to grips with changing lifestyles. It is apparent to most social researchers and practitioners that we as a society need to build more caregiving supports into our social structure. In the meantime, older people and their families will often seek social services because they are facing the problem of how to manage the ongoing support of an aging family member.

SOCIAL SERVICES

The aim of social work, according to Rosenfeld, is "to match resources with needs to increase the 'goodness of fit' between them" (1983, p. 186). In order to establish such a fit, the older person must be helped to recognize the need and society must provide adequate resources to supply the need. Meeting each of these criteria poses a challenge for the social worker.

This is a society in which entitlements and benefits are psychologically associated with welfare or with some residual programs in society for meeting needs. We have a view of need that is associated with weakness and disadvantage. Social workers frequently are confronted by clients who "don't believe in Medicaid" or "don't need to go to a senior center" or "don't want Meals-on-Wheels." We have a deeply rooted bias in this country that supports the myth of rugged individualism and decries any form of dependency. However obvious it may be that changing times require new solutions, people are likely to remain steadfast in this belief.

One of the current and ongoing debates in the delivery of services focuses on means testing for benefits. For example, should eligibility for Social Security require means testing? Many services provided through the network under the authority of the Older Americans Act and other federal legislation do not require means testing. Lunch and recreation programs at senior centers and Meals-on-Wheels are open to all regardless of income. Social Security and Medicare are generally viewed as entitlement programs because of the mandatory contributions from wages associated with these programs. However, an individual's total contribution does not meet the costs of the benefits generally received throughout retirement, and so, it is not entirely logical for an individual who receives Social Security and Medicare to argue against the morality of accepting Medicaid funds for nursing care because of the social stigma of "being on welfare." One pressing problem of many older people flows from unrealistic planning based on obstinately held and sometimes contradictory beliefs. They often must be helped to acknowledge their need for, and right to, benefits. At the same time, the entitlement and assistance programs may not be able to meet the growing demand for services and benefits. Will the Social Security system and Medicare be able to support the growing need for long-term care?

This brings us to a second part of the social work function in the field of aging—the obligation to participate in organizational and institutional efforts to plan and promote financially and socially responsible social programs. The social worker not only must help the individual use services but must also help bring the social and health service systems into sync with people's needs. Two ways in which the social worker can advocate for the needs of vulnerable older adults are program planning and participation on legislative task force committees of such professional associations as the National Association for Social Workers or the Gerontological Society of America.

Some groups of aged people are needier than others and require greater attention from the gerontological social work community. These are individuals whose families are geographically distant or otherwise unavailable; whose families have rejected or abandoned them; who live in rural areas (people in rural areas tend to have lower incomes, poorer physical health and less mobility than their urban counterparts); and those who have historically been excluded from the system. Older adults in minority groups do not receive a share of social benefits in proportion to their needs, in spite of the false assumption that utilization of social welfare service is high among minority groups (Cuellar & Weeks, 1980).

Finally, among older adults there are certain common social losses that may create a need for social work assistance. Retirement, loss of spouse, decline of health, economic decline, and loss of friends may all serve as triggers for use of social services. Sometimes an elderly individual has not prepared adequately for loss of a paycheck or for impending physical frailty. Sometimes an older person may experience the death of a spouse and need help adjusting to life as a single adult. These losses may result in negative feelings, ranging from impaired self-esteem to grief, depression, dependency, which may serve as the impetus for seeking help. An outreach worker in a senior center, or an adult service worker in a community center, or a social worker in a senior housing office is probably as likely to encounter these feelings in performing casework, administrative, or programmatic functions as is a psychiatric social worker in a mental health clinic. This underscores the need for comprehensive assessment in working with older people and the importance of close coordination of social and health services.

HEALTH SERVICES

The incidence of many chronic mental and physical conditions increases with age. Among the mental disorders that increase with age are depression and certain cognitive mental disorders, such as Alzheimer's disease and related dementias and language disorders. In addition, chronic diseases now outrank acute conditions as health risks for older adults.

The chronic conditions most frequently reported in persons over age 65 are:

Arthritis (49 percent)

Hypertension (37 percent)

Hearing impairments (32 percent)

Heart diseases (30 percent)

Other disorders among the top ten chronic conditions are orthopedic impairments, sinusitis, cataracts, diabetes, visual impairment and tinnitus. In addition, the older person accumulates an increasing number of functional limitations resulting from age-related changes in organ systems, including mobility problems. Sensory changes also occur frequently with old age, including changes in vision, hearing, taste, smell, and tactile ability (Hooyman & Kiyak, 1993).

Mortality rates indicate that the major causes of death among people over 65 are heart disease, cancer, and stroke (cerebrovascular accident or CVA); U.S. Census, 1993).

The primary ways in which these health needs affect the need for social services relate to "quality of life" issues, health insurance, and requirements for long term care. For example, an older individual may need help setting the terms of a health proxy agreement or "do not resuscitate" order. When an older person is faced with incapacity, sorting out priorities for continued care can easily become fraught with conflict. The older individual may need help determining a long term financial plan. Deciding to which child to give power of attorney may be complicated and stressful for an older adult, for example.

Older people will seek help from psychotherapists and religious leaders, in addition to physicians, physical therapists, and nutritionists, in their efforts to adapt to limitations in functioning.

They often seek the assistance of social workers, financial planners, and lawyers in planning for incapacity.

The presenting problems of older people are seldom discrete; rather, these problems demonstrate the connections among mental health, physical health, social concerns and financial concerns. Whether or not they are looking for help with the needs that are associated with increased frailty, one thing is certain. Every older adult will experience some medical or sensory disorder that will cause him or her to seek a physician's attention. An astute physician will understand the complexities surrounding the individual's presenting health problem and make appropriate referrals for ancillary social and psychological services.

The gerontological social worker in a health setting will often be presented with the need for an individual and his or her family to arrange for long term care, ranging from home health care to placement in a home for adults or a nursing home. Coverage for home care under Medicare is extremely limited, necessitating high out-of-pocket expenses or application for community Medicaid. The Medicaid application process is extremely complex and may involve transfers of assets, which may compound the older person's vulnerability to abuse. Placement in a nursing home or adult residence for long term care is equally complex and has financial, legal, and emotional aspects that must be carefully evaluated. All of these matters are fraught with stress for the older person who faces increased dependency at the hands of health providers, a spouse or children. All of these matters have ethical implications, sometimes requiring the social worker to assume the role of advocate for the client. The social worker is obligated to protect the rights of his or her clients in situations where these rights are being threatened. As indicated earlier, the social worker in a health setting is likely to be involved in decisions having to do with quality of life and health care. Relatively new legislation that supports the right of the individual to make his or her own decisions about treatment, (e.g., "do not resuscitate" or a health proxy) in spite of lost mental capacity often must be explained to people at times when they are most frightened and are feeling most threatened. The social worker's sensitivity is critical in promoting people's understanding of their choices and their use of the options that are available to empower them. Illness and functional impairment are difficult to cope with in any case. Often the social worker is the one person in whom an older individual can confide his or her fears, without feeling judged. In fact, nonjudgmental listening may be the social worker's greatest tool in helping his or her clients. The art and skill of listening to someone in physical or mental pain is the essence of helping and healing through communication.

LEGAL SERVICES

Most social work services have legal ramifications. The reverse is also true. A person seeking the services of a lawyer will usually need help with the psychological or social ramifications of the legal issue. This is the reason lawyers and social workers have been open to forming working partnerships. Gerontological practice is at the cutting edge of collaborative activity between the two disciplines.

Just as social losses are associated with mental health problems, and concerns about long term financial planning are associated with physical or mental decline, legal matters—ranging from eligibility for entitlements such as Social Security to planning one's estate—frequently have implications for health and social matters. The issues that will draw an older individual or family member to a private lawyer or legal aid office generally fall into one of two categories: (1) financial or (2) health related.

Financial matters will run the gamut from planning for retirement to planning for incapacity to estate planning. Health-related matters include the legalities involved in the preparation of advance directives (e.g., health proxies and "do-not-resuscitate" orders); applications to extended care facilities or application for home care services; and applications for benefits such as Medicaid. Although older people are frequently victims of physical or mental abuse, abuse is actually less likely to be a presenting problem than some hidden agony, which a lawyer or social worker may uncover in the assessment process.

An important role for social workers in any area of practice is to help people acknowledge the need to plan for retirement. Social workers in the field of aging must often deal with individuals who have not planned adequately or who lack the resources to have planned effectively. Women and minorities are most prone to encounter financial problems as they age, because Social Security benefits are linked to total individual federal tax payments, and pensions are mostly available in companies or organizations that primarily employ White men. An important responsibility for social advocacy flows from this inequitable situation. The social worker is not only responsible for providing help to individual clients but is also obligated to promote policies and practices aimed at combating social injustices, such as unequal employment practices. Thus, the social worker in a legal setting, such as a legal aid office, should be prepared to participate in activities aimed at affecting legislative policy. The professional function is characterized by its emphasis on helping both the individual in need and the organizations that exist to serve those needs.

RELIGIONS, COMMUNITY, AND LABOR MARKET

Older people tend to be religious. Both men and women report that spirituality is related to their sense of well-being (Hooyman & Kiyak, 1993). However, although churches in the United States have developed youth ministries, youth programs, and family programs, services for older adults are scarce. Churches and synagogues are not traditional social service providers but houses of worship; still social agencies and religious organizations appeal to many of the same human needs for emotional and spiritual fulfillment.

The term *joint venture* describes the integrating of services between two separate organizations. Joint ventures are increasingly popular organizational arrangements in health services delivery and this concept has applicability for the delivery of social and religious services. Social service agencies can provide outreach services in churches and synagogues for the purpose of identifying the needs of older congregants and to assist in the development of church- or synagogue-based recreational and support services, such as respite programs for caregivers of Alzheimer's patients. The space between religious needs and emotional needs is very narrow. Community social service agencies traditionally respond to a large range of health, educational, social, and recreational needs. The continuum of services for older people includes senior volunteer programs, community center social and political advocacy groups, and continuing educational programs—in addition to the entire range of health-related nutritional, physical, educational and caregiver and patient support services. Social workers have opportunities to create joint programs on many different fronts. Planning and administrative expertise, including skill in collaboration, are essential elements of community-based social work practice.

The human resource departments of businesses and corporations represent a novel arena for social work practice. Reductions in the number of younger people in the labor market in the post–baby boom era have opened opportunities for nontraditional employees, such as older workers, disabled workers, female workers, and minority workers. The transition to this new work force is slow, and social workers in employee assistance programs can still expect to have to deal with obstacles in the recruitment of older individuals as well as discriminatory layoff practices. In addition, older people will need to be accommodated in certain practical ways if their return to work is to be successful. Older people need to be assured of safe and convenient transportation to and from work. They will probably require retraining in use of modern office technology, and attention will have to be given to such environmental considerations as glare and background noise (Nathanson & O'Rourke, 1994). The increased number of older people in the business community creates a whole new set of technical activities that relate to the development of human resources. New positions for social workers in corporations are adding to the array of traditional social work occupations in community service and organization.

In chapter 3 we have defined the scope of the needs associated with various aspects of older adults' functioning. Each of these needs calls for different individual and group interventions. Some social work roles emphasize the delivery of casework services, whereas others, such as the role of community organizer, emphasize a broader focus on social reform or change. The principles presented in Chapter 2 are given different relative weights, in different settings, depending on the needs of individual clients or client groups and the mission or purpose of the agency. In the following chapters, we attempt to demonstrate an application of our integrative methodology to specific case examples.

REFERENCES

Atchley, R. C. (1991). *Social forces and aging.* Wadsworth, CA: Wadsworth.

Cuellar, J. B. & Weeks, J. (1980). Minority elderly Americans: A profile for area agencies on aging, executive summary. AOA grant 90-A-1667. Allied Home Health Association. San Diego, CA: Author.

Hendricks, J., & Hendricks, D. C. (1986). *Aging in mass society.* Boston: Little Brown.

Hooyman, N., & Kyack, A. H. (1993). *Social gerontology. (3rd ed.).* Boston: Allyn and Bacon.

Nathanson, I. L., & O'Rourke, K. (1994). The job interests, work incentives and perceived barriers and limitations to employment of a group of older trainees. *Journal of Gerontological Social Work, 21* (3/4).

Rosenfeld, J. (1983). The domain and expertise of social work: A conceptualization. *Social Work, 28,* 186–191.

Tirrito, T., & Nathanson, I. (1994, Spring). Ethnic differences in caregiving: Adult daughters and elderly mothers, *AFFILIA, 9* (1), 71–84.

U.S. Bureau of the Census. (1993). *Statistical abstract of the United States* (113th ed.). Washington, DC: U.S. Government Printing Office.

CHAPTER 4

Gerontological Psychiatric Social Work Practice

A n older person's social experience often is characterized by loss—loss of health, loss of job, loss of friends, and loss of spouse are common examples of personal and social losses. Those individuals who must reconcile themselves to the changing demands of a generally shrinking social experience very often seek assistance from a social worker. These individuals may select from a wide field of private practitioners and mental health agencies that represent psychiatric social work services. This chapter discusses the role of the psychiatric social worker and the combination of generic and specialized knowledge that guides psychiatric social workers' performance of their functions. The chapter includes two case examples, one representing the application of principles of psychiatric social work in a traditional agency structure; the other illustrating the application of these concepts in a solo practice.

WHAT IS GERONTOLOGICAL PSYCHIATRIC SOCIAL WORK PRACTICE?

Gerontological social work is social work practiced with older people and gerontological psychiatric social work is social work practiced with older people in a mental health setting.

Adherents of functional social work and adherents to the psychosocial orientation, which has its roots in the diagnostic approach, would part ways over the issue of whether or not social work in general or gerontological psychiatric social work can be practiced on a solo, fee-for-service practice basis. The traditional functionalist orientation would dismiss solo practice from any definition of social work, because it is not connected to an institutionalized structure. The psychosocial orientation seemingly would allow solo practice within the scope of professional social work, as long as the social worker includes a focus on the social environment as part of the plan for assessment and treatment of clients.

The meaning of *social advocacy* is somewhat different for those who focus on the individual as the primary instrument of social change and those who believe that the social environment is as critical as individual growth, if not more so, in promoting the social good. Rather than get into the nuances of these different meanings, we will simply express our particular bias: To be social work, social work must be practiced in an agency framework. However, many social workers are in fact involved in solo practice with older people. Therefore, we would like to offer an understanding of what might distinguish solo social work practice from other psychotherapeutic approaches, and so we have developed the concept of *professionally informed* solo casework or group work. This is a recognition of the common generic underpinnings of social work in all fields, including solo practice. Still, we warn against the notion (which might seem to flow from this concept) that the practice is defined by the practitioner: "If a social worker's doing the job, it's social work." This thinking would go too far toward another extreme. To repeat, we would suggest that the best social work is carried out in an agency, but we acknowledge that solo practice retains many of the ideological and technical aspects of the profession. It is these commonalities that we will define through the use of our case examples.

GENERIC PRINCIPLES OF GERONTOLOGICAL PSYCHIATRIC SOCIAL WORK

The following principles reiterate and expand on the generic principles outlined in chapter 1.

1. Diagnosis or assessment of the client must be comprehensive and must include mental status, physical health, spiritual health, and legal, financial, and social condition.
2. Diagnosis or understanding of the client's need is most effective when related to the use of a particular psychiatric service in the context of the client's relationship with the worker.

3. The agency function (or contract with the client) gives direction and focus to the work.

4. Conscious use of administrative skills (e.g., use of time, policy, and strategic planning) promotes more effective delivery of service.

5. The relationship between the client and the worker, as defined by the function or contract, flows from the client's relationship with the agency, the total client system, or both, and can be used to promote the interests of the particular client and the interests of the client's representative social group.

6. Conscious use of collaborative skills promotes more effective delivery of service.

Our bias toward agency-based practice is reflected in our basic adherence to Smalley's generic paradigm. We have expanded these principles to demonstrate their applicability to solo practice, but the basic principles remain the same. The contract or work agreement between the solo practitioner and the client provides the focus and direction to the work. The emphasis on relationship as a key to movement in the process recognizes that object relations have a relatively greater influence than diagnostic interpretation on movement or growth. We support the client's centrality to the process of defining his or her purposes in the context of the agency function or within the limits established by the worker. We underscore the importance of the secondary professional processes of administration and collaboration to effective work with older clients. Comprehensive assessment is fundamental to social work with older people, regardless of the specificity of the agency function or the worker-client contract. A mental health professional cannot limit his or her assessment of need to the client's use of a psychiatric social work service but must assess the full scope of the client's need as it pertains to the use of a range of health and social services. The worker is not specific in his or her diagnosis of need even though he or she is specific in the definition of the particular task. The client is referred to other agencies or individuals as appropriate. Coordination is part of the gerontological psychiatric social worker's role.

THE WORKER'S ROLE IN THE ENTRY PHASE

What are the specific tasks that constitute the role of the gerontological psychiatric social worker? We first introduced the concepts outlined below in an earlier book (Tirrito, Nathanson, & Langer, 1996). Here, we elaborate on the principles outlined in the model for counseling.

The psychiatric social worker who works with older people has specific tasks to perform in different phases of the helping process, and the entry phase of the helping process is marked by two significant activities. The first involves the (biopsychosocial) diagnosis or general assessment of the client's need; and the second involves establishing a contract with the client that defines the scope of the work to be done together.

THE FUNCTIONAL AGE ASSESSMENT

The social worker begins by taking a complete medical history and conducts an assessment of the client's functional capabilities and limitations in managing activities of daily living. As part of this comprehensive assessment, the client's support system is evaluated. The social worker assesses the family's potential for providing informal caregiving if necessary. The client's recent losses must be evaluated. Did a recent bout of ill health or loss of spouse occur that would help to explain any current deficits in mental or social functioning? How is the individual functioning relative to other members of his or her age cohort? A disparity between this individual's cognitive or social functioning and that of the average individual in the age cohort suggests the possibility of any combination of problems ranging from physical illness to emotional disturbance to organic brain disease. The individual's psychological profile should include an assessment of conflicts. Does the individual suffer from internal conflicts, such as guilt, or are most of the perceived problems related to limitations in the environment (e.g., financial difficulties or lack of social contacts.) This profile includes a description of the nature of the defenses: lower-level (e.g., denial or projection) versus higher-level (e.g., rationalization or sublimation). The nature of the anxiety (free-floating, rigidly bound, unconscious) and the type of depression (lifelong or reactive) should also be included in the profile. Also critical to the assessment is the nature of the patient's object relations (self-gratifying, mutually gratifying).

In other words, as with any age cohort, the client's character structure should be assessed so that the presenting problem is placed in some meaningful context. Does a widow who is still in mourning 3 years after the death of her spouse have a characteristic tendency toward depression? If so, she may need help from the social worker with separation issues, as would any younger person expressing a pathological reaction to a loss.

The assessment or differential diagnosis focuses on separating out biological, social, and psychological factors in determining whether an individual is struggling with lifelong emotional conflicts, has a possible untreated biochemical imbalance or medical condition, or is demonstrating a normal emotional reaction to a loss. Within the functional orientation, the initial psychiatric social work plan will depend on the nature of the client's specific set of social needs—again, as with any age group.

CONTRACT

The contract represents an agreement between the client and the social worker regarding the nature of the work to be done, and wherever possible, the time frame in which the work is to be accomplished. In the functional framework, the contract would represent the common ground between the client's need and the agency's purpose. The agency provides an outside limitation on the nature of the work and also, in a psychological sense, a fulcrum around which the worker and the client may move without getting lost. The worker must mediate between the requirements of the client and those of the agency in promoting the effectiveness of the agency in providing for some social good. Both the individual client and the agency have the potential to grow as a result of the client's encounter with the worker.

In a psychiatric or mental health setting, the role of the worker will vary according to the assigned task. An intake worker is responsible only for making an initial assessment. A worker in an outpatient mental health clinic may be charged with the responsibility for providing clients with long-term help or perhaps for coordinating aftercare service for newly discharged inpatients of psychiatric hospitals. An inpatient psychiatric social worker may be primarily responsible for discharge planning. The agency defines the role, and it is specific.

In the solo practice arena, clients will go to social workers for "psychotherapy" or perhaps for management of geriatric care (coordination of services). The purpose of the interaction is defined by the worker and the client. No agency is involved. However, the contract is still an option for the solo practitioner in defining the scope of the work and focusing the efforts of the worker and client. It is important to note that most older people do not enter "therapy" with the intention of changing their characters or personalities, and this makes a task-focused approach generally more practical than a strict psychoanalytic or diagnostic approach. A task-focused approach does not obviate the importance of forming an attachment with the client, or of exploring the emotional and interpersonal implications of the individual's thoughts and behaviors. It is merely recommended as a general guide to understanding the role of the worker in the individual practice setting and the nature of the worker-client contract. It also provides a connection to a generic functional model of social work practice.

CASE EXAMPLE 1: APPLICATION OF INTEGRATED METHODOLOGY WITH A DEPRESSED OLDER ADULT

Case example 1 is provided to illustrate the generic principles identified above. The case highlights the importance of comprehensive assessment and the relationship of diagnosis to the use of a particular psychiatric service. The case also illustrates the relationship of the helping process to the agency function.

> Adele Harris is a 67-year-old White female whose husband Stanley, 72, was admitted to Riverview Nursing Home after suffering a massive stroke. He has been a resident for the past 3 months and shows little sign of improvement. His prognosis for recovery of motor and ADL functions is described as poor by his wife, who expects him to require skilled nursing care for the rest of his life. Adele has been visiting her husband almost daily and has shown signs of emotional distress, including weeping, lack of animation in her voice, and neglect of her appearance. The social worker on the unit to which Stanley is assigned approached Adele to discuss her adjustment to Stanley's physical condition, and Adele broke down in tears, claiming that she has difficulty getting out of bed each morning and would like to die. The social worker referred Adele to an individual and family counseling center in the community. The following process recording represents Adele's first meeting with the social worker at the center.

FIRST INTERVIEW

Worker: Adele, tell me what you've been experiencing lately.

Adele: I just want to die since Stanley was admitted to the nursing home. I feel as though my life is over. I recognize that this may seem selfish to you, but I can't deal with the loneliness.

Worker: What is it about the loneliness that is distressing to you?

Adele: I don't want to give the impression that my husband and I had the best relationship; but we got along, and I felt he was there for me. Now I feel I'm all alone. I know it sounds ridiculous, since my children live upstairs in the same house as I do, but it's not the same. I have nobody to go shopping with, have dinner with, talk to....I really can't stand being alone.

Worker: Have you ever lived alone, Adele?

Adele: No. I got married at 19. I know I'm not acting rationally. I've always been a dependent type. I'm very needy.

Worker: How do you think you're needy?

Adele: I can't be alone. I was the baby in my family. I can't take care of myself.

Worker: You say you were the baby. How many children were in your family?

Adele: There was my older sister, she's 7 years older than I am. I have an older brother—6 years older—and a twin brother.

Worker: What's your relationship like with them now?

Adele: I'm very close with my sister, but she lives upstate. I speak with my brothers pretty regularly, but we only see each other occasionally.

Worker: How do you feel you have been babied?

Adele: I don't know. I just never lived alone.

Worker: Did you feel your mother babied you?

Adele: No. Actually, I was just there. She was more attached to my older sister. I guess I wasn't really babied. I never really went to anyone for anything. I just started to feel dependent as I got older. I started to get scared after my brother-in law died about 6 years ago. I started thinking about getting old and being alone.

Worker: And what is it about being alone?

Adele: Just that. I know I sound stupid; but. I don't know what to do with myself. When I was with my husband we'd do things together.

Worker: What things?

Adele: Everything..the movies, visit friends. I can't be with my married friends like we used to be.

Worker: Why not?

Adele: My friends' husbands resent it. They don't say anything, but I know I'm a fifth wheel. I can't be alone. I know I'm immature, but I just don't want to be alone....and I am alone!

Worker: So now your worst fear seems to have been realized?

Adele: (Begins to weep.) Yes, that's it. I wouldn't say I always felt like this. I used to make people laugh. I was the life of the party. People used to like to have me around. Now, my children look at me as if I'm some kind of wounded animal. I hate that, but I can't help it. The only reason I don't kill myself is that I don't want to be a burden to my children.

Worker: Have you given serious thought to killing yourself?

Adele: Yes.

Worker: How would you do it?

Adele: I would turn on the gas in my son's car and do it that way. I thought about taking pills. The doctor gave me Prozac, but I don't know how many to take. I don't want to be left like a vegetable.

Worker: You must be very angry to be considering killing yourself?

Adele: Oh yes, I am so angry. I am so resentful. My husband and I never asked for much. He worked as a machinist, and I worked for a clothing manufacturer. I was a clerk. We made a modest living, but now between our small savings and Social Security, we could afford to pay our bills and take a little vacation once in a while. We were planning a trip to California when he had the stroke. I feel so cheated. I look at couples, and I feel so jealous. I was never like that. I just can't see any way out of this.

Worker:	What do you see happening to you down the road?
Adele:	That's just it. I see my life going on the way it is right now. That's why I want to end it.
Worker:	Do you imagine you will always feel as badly as you feel right now?
Adele:	Yes, and I can't go on feeling like this. I'm lonely. I feel as if I'm not even here. I know it sounds crazy.
Worker:	It doesn't sound crazy. Who'd want to go on feeling the way you do right now? Adele, before we go on, let me just mention to you that I'd like you to be evaluated for medication, because I think some medication might help you right now.
Adele:	But I went to my doctor, who gave me the Prozac. I didn't like the effect. It made me jittery, and I was afraid I'd get sick from it.
Worker:	You were afraid you'd get sick! The way you're feeling, what difference would that make? You're talking about killing yourself!
Adele:	You're right. I just didn't know what I'd do if I got sick and I was alone.
Worker:	Adele, I know we've just met, but do you think you could start to think of me as someone who is there for you if you're feeling frightened? That way you could try the medication, if a psychiatrist recommends it, and you could tell me any symptoms you might get. You might not feel as alone.
Adele:	Oh, would you mind if I called you? I wouldn't want you to get sick of me.
Worker:	The way you feel your children are getting sick of you?
Adele:	I just feel so abandoned, and it's nobody's fault.
Worker:	Let's say we could do something for the way you're feeling. If you did feel a little better, can you imagine anything that might help you feel as though life could have some pleasure in it again? Is there anything that might give you some hope, Adele?
Adele:	You mean if I didn't feel so bad? Well, I really wish I had a friend who was widowed. Then I might feel that we could console each other and maybe spend time together. I wish I had somebody to do things with.
Worker:	What a perfectly reasonable desire! Do you think that would be impossible, let's say, if you weren't as depressed?
Adele:	I think I would like that.
Worker:	I think I can help you with that. You know, Adele, you're going through a mourning stage, even though your husband is still alive. You've lost your companion. You must expect to go through a painful adjustment.
Adele:	It must sound terrible, but I wish my husband had died. He would have been better off, and I think I would be better off.
Worker:	Your situation is very difficult because you've lost your old life and it's hard to imagine anything changing for the better.
Adele:	(In tears.) Please don't abandon me.
Worker:	Then don't abandon us. We have a lot of work to do to make a life for you that you can live with.

Comments on the First Interview

This case illustrates many of the principles of the generic integrative methodology presented in this book. First of all, the client, Adele Harris, is referred from one agency (the nursing home) to an agency whose function is to provide individual and family counseling. The social worker at the nursing home had a clear sense of her responsibilities and the limitations of these responsibilities. The counseling center provides counseling for different life crises or developmental difficulties facing individuals and families and therefore has appropriate resources (including psychiatric backup) to serve the needs of individuals such as Adele, who is suffering from an emotional problem associated with a life crisis. The worker's emphasis on defining a focus for the work with this client reflects the problem-solving orientation that suits the needs of an older client, without disregarding the feelings of the client and need for emotional support.

The case further illustrates the importance of the psycho-social assessment process. The Multidisciplinary Screening Instrument (MSI, Tirrito, Nathanson, & Langer, 1996) is given in Appendix A of the present book and should be used in any intake process. The gerontological social worker should screen for medical, legal, and financial deficits in clients' functioning as a matter of course. Although we did not represent this in the preceding dialogue, a general assessment would include such a comprehensive screen.

Psychoanalytic understanding is crucial to the client's assessment. Is the client's grief normal or a reflection of a fragile ego structure? The worker's questions are geared to determining the meaning of dependency for this client. Whether the client is suffering from a traumatic reaction to a crisis or from lifelong dependency problems of an extremely needy individual is not settled. The diagnosis is being made in the context of the interaction between client and worker as defined by the individual's presenting problem and the agency's function. The significance of the agency-based service is reflected in the fact that the client is not only an individual being served, but a member of a class of clients with similar needs. Maybe the worker will establish a discussion group for women living alone, as an institutional response to individual clients' expressed concerns for meaningful social contact.

COMMUNICATION SKILLS

There are a variety of different communication skills associated with the implementation of the social work role. These include the following: partialization, generalization, reflection, reaching for the negative feelings under the positive, reaching for the positive feelings under the negative, engendering a revival of a feeling, and validating a feeling. They are defined as follows.

- *Partialization:* Process of breaking down a generalized statement into its components, (E.g., What do you mean, "The whole world treats you badly"?)
- *Generalization:* Process of identifying a pattern to behaviors or statements of feeling or belief. (E.g., Whenever you arrive here you always have some criticism to make of me, what do you make of that?)
- *Reflection:* Process of providing a mirror of a statement that represents a slightly deeper reflection of its meaning. (E.g., You said you are tired of going to work. Are you saying you don't intend to keep your job? Another example might be: You said you'd prefer to be by yourself. Are you asking me to leave?)
- *Reaching for the negative feelings under the positive:* Process of encouraging the expression of negative feelings that might underlie an individual's positive statement. (E.g., You love "everything" about the residential community?)
- *Reaching for the positive feelings under the negative:* Process of encouraging the expression of positive feelings that may underlie an individual's negative statement. (E.g., You hate "everything" about the nursing home?)
- *Engendering a revival of a feeling:* Process of prompting an individual to recapture a feeling associated with a past experience. (E.g., What were you thinking when you decided not to show up at the last session? Another example might be: Who was so hard on you that you always expect harsh criticism?)
- *Validating and empathizing:* Process of acknowledging that the feelings being expressed are reasonable. (E.g., It doesn't sound crazy. Who'd want to go on living, feeling the way you do?)

These and other verbal and nonverbal techniques are used to achieve the specific objectives defined by the worker in the context of the agency's function and the client's need. Some of these skills are intended to clarify the client's verbal expression; they are based on the principle that the more differentiated the clients' ability to express themselves, the less ambiguous their focus and the less disorganized their personality and behavior will be. Some of the skills are intended to foster an openness to growth or movement in areas where the client is resistant because of previous interpersonal losses or failures. In essence, the social worker asks to be told about past pain that may be obstructing the client's progress at this time and in this place. Some of the skills are intended to demonstrate understanding and acceptance of the client's feelings and perceptions. The function or purpose of the work defined in the contract is the pivot or focus of the interaction—meaning communication—between the worker and the client. In the functional approach, the worker sets out, not to change the client's character, but only to achieve an established purpose in association with the client. The fact that both may be changed in the process is not so much incidental to the process of helping as implicit in it.

Lawrence Shulman (1992) distinguishes between skills that are related to helping the client manage *feelings* and those that are related to helping the client manage *problems*. Regarding the former—feelings—he mentions the following skills:

- Reaching inside of silences
- Putting the client's feelings into words
- Displaying understanding of the client's feelings
- Sharing the worker's feelings

Regarding the latter—problems—he notes the following skills:

- Clarifying the worker's purpose and role
- Reaching for feedback from the client
- Partializing the client's concerns
- Supporting the client in taboo areas

In case example 1, "supporting the client in taboo areas" might mean (for example) helping Adele make the choice not to have her husband discharged home under her supervision.

Shulman points out that it is is not the skills that define the professional; rather, their functions or roles distinguish one type of professional from another. He also addresses the connection between the client's ability to manage feelings and to manage problems, since how we feel has a powerful effect on how we act, and vice versa.

QUESTIONS FOR DISCUSSION: THE WORKER'S ROLE AND COMMUNICATION SKILLS IN CASE 1

1. In the case of Adele Harris, is the worker successful at establishing a contract with the client?
2. How is Adele's age important in understanding her psychodynamics?
3. What generic social work tasks is the worker addressing in this first interview?
4. How does the worker use the concept of relationship to achieve specific objectives?
5. Would the interview have gone differently with a younger client?
6. Does the worker use any specific communication skills?
7. What questions would be important to ensure a comprehensive biopsychosocial assessment?
8. What generic principles of gerontological social work practice are represented in this interview?
9. What should be the worker's focus with Adele's family?
10. How should the worker follow up on the suicide threat?

CASE 1, SECOND INTERVIEW

The following excerpt is taken from the second interview with Adele one week later and illustrates the worker's effort to clarify the meaning of Adele's expressed neediness, and also to evaluate Adele's ego structure (e.g., reality testing, intelligence, defenses). The diagnostic information is useful in terms of establishing realistic goals for the client, determining the need for the worker to assume the role of "self-object" (Kohut, in Greenberg & Mitchell, 1983) as well as "real object" (Blanck & Blanck, 1974) in relation to the client, who may need help with separation issues and with coping. The "self-object" is an individual who provides experiences necessary for the gradual development of the self through empathic responsiveness to the infant's and child's needs. The "real object" reinforces the real perception of external experience through mechanisms such as setting limits, and what Schwartz describes as "lending a vision and projecting one's own feelings" about the struggles in which the client and worker are engaged.

The following excerpt also includes an illustration of the worker's effort to evaluate the family's supportive potential.

Adele: I spoke with my sister, and when I mentioned the possibility of my coming to stay with her, she reacted very badly. She basically told me that I wasn't welcome.

Worker: How would you explain her reaction?

Adele: I think she thinks I would be a burden, smother her.... But she should know better.

Worker: When your sister called me about you, she also used the word *baby* to describe you.... Where does this idea about you being a baby come from?

Adele: I was the youngest.

Worker: What else does it mean to you?

Adele: I don't know; maybe she thinks I'll be needy because I always had trouble with change, like when my children left for college. I didn't know how I'd deal with it.... I cried when my children got married.... I wanted everything to stay the same, but I coped because I had Stanley....I thought I'd always have Stanley. I was so surprised when Stanley had a stroke. I just couldn't believe it.

Worker: Adele, how come Stanley's stroke came as such a surprise? You know he has very high blood pressure....it puzzles me that you were so surprised....at his age. You never considered the possibility?

Adele: No, because Stanley always took such care of himself. He exercised, ate well, went to the doctor all the time....He was such a vital man.... I just never considered it....I thought I'd go first, even though I'm younger, I guess I'm crazy...I am crazy. I just didn't want to imagine life without him.

Worker: I'd like to know a little more about Stanley's condition. Is he able to communicate?

Adele: He talks; he understands everything.... He just can't walk; he needs help with using the toilet, washing, eating.

Worker: Is he getting rehab?

Adele: My son doesn't think he's getting the right rehab. They seem to be cutting back just when he's showing some progress—starting to bend his legs, to pull himself up in bed.

Worker: Where did you get the idea he will be confined to a nursing home for the remainder of his life?

Adele: I don't see enough progress.

Worker: Would you be willing to let me talk with your son about your husband's condition? Would your son talk to me?

Adele: Oh, of course. We've been thinking of having Stanley transferred someplace where he'd get better treatment. We haven't been sure what to do.

Worker: Adele, I just don't understand why you've written Stanley off in terms of his potential for improvement, now that you've explained his condition to me.

Adele:	I had hope at the beginning, but I just stopped hoping because I didn't see enough progress.
Worker:	Was it difficult to hope?
Adele:	Oh yes, I can't deal with any more disappointment. I'm too upset, too frightened to consider anything being different.
Worker:	It could get worse as well as better.
Adele:	It can't get worse than it is now. What do I do when I get home, what do I do with myself when I get that hollow pain and I feel claustrophobic and I just want to crawl out of my skin?
Worker:	You really are suffering. Right now I want you to see Dr. Marks. I am confident she can prescribe something that will help with these feelings. Then we have a lot to sort out together. I think I can help you with your loneliness and any adjustments you might have to make in your life. I'd like to speak with your son about Stanley, and in the meantime you just have to bear with the process. Do you think you can?
Adele:	I guess I have no choice but to try.

In the second interview, the worker delved more deeply into the client's perceptions and feelings in order to better clarify the level of the client's psychological functioning. The worker has assessed the client as not strong enough to deal with the issues related to her husband's long term care, but recognizes the connection between Stanley's prognosis and the client's immediate concerns and makes an effort to engage Adele's son in this aspect of the assessment and helping process.

QUESTIONS FOR DISCUSSION: CASE 1, SECOND INTERVIEW

1. What type of defense is predominant in Adele's ego functioning?

2. What does an understanding of Adele's ego functioning contribute to the worker's assessment and planning within a functional or task-oriented framework?

3. Who is the client?

4. If the understanding is that Adele is the client, then how does one explain the worker's relationship with the family members?

5. Is the contract clear? Would it help to further clarify the nature of the work for the client?

6. If the client has separation issues and dependency needs, how will this influence the nature of the work?

CASE EXAMPLE 2: AN ALZHEIMER'S PATIENT AND HIS CAREGIVER

Michael Kramer is an 84-year-old White man who was referred to a privately employed social work practitioner by a psychiatrist who has been treating Michael for symptoms of dementia and depression. Michael is a retired certified public accountant who lives with his wife in Greenwich, Connecticut. His wife is a retired art professor who gives private art instruction on a part-time basis. Both Michael and his wife were referred for help in coordinating a plan for long term care for Michael. The initial contact was made by the wife Carla, an 81-year-old White woman. The following represents the first telephone conversation between Carla and the social worker.

Carla: I was referred to you by Dr. Mansfield, who believes that you have something to offer my husband and me in the way of help. I have some questions for you because I can't understand how you can help us.

Worker: Please ask whatever you'd like.

Carla: What is it you do?

Worker: To a certain extent it depends on what you need, but in general I am a certified social worker who specializes in working with older people in regard to issues and problems that are typical of the age group.

Carla: My husband and I have a problem: Michael's been depressed since he retired 2 years ago, and he seems to be getting worse; but that's why we go to Dr. Mansfield. What do you do that's different? He hasn't done anything but prescribe various medications that don't work.

Worker: What reason did Dr. Mansfield give for referring you to me?

Carla: He said you help people hook up with any services that they may need. What kind of services?

Worker: Well, that would explain part of what I do. I would evaluate your need for home care or your financial status—your eligibility for any assistance. I would also assess how you and your husband are coping with his condition.

Carla: We have a lawyer, so we don't need you for that. We don't need home care. Can you help Michael with his depression?

Worker: Is that what you understand his problem to be—depression?

Carla: Nobody seems to know. He's been to many different doctors; nobody has been able to do anything for him. Now I feel he's slipping further into a noncommunicative state.

Worker: I could speak with him and see if I could recommend some help. But what makes you say it's depression? Who told you that it was?

Carla:	Dr. Mansfield thinks Michael has something organically wrong with him; but I don't think he has Alzheimer's disease. He understands me perfectly.
Worker:	Is it a concern of yours?
Carla:	Wouldn't anybody be concerned? Would you know if he has Alzheimer's?
Worker:	I could get an idea and discuss it with Dr. Mansfield. What would it mean to you if I offered an opinion?
Carla:	Could you do anything for him?
Worker:	If he has a dementia, I can't do anything to make him well, but I might be able to help him function as well as he can. But I can't really know anything unless I speak with your husband directly. Sometimes I help a wife cope with a husband's failing health.
Carla:	Well, I don't need any help right now. I'm coping. Maybe you could suggest something for Michael, however, which is my only concern.
Worker:	All right, then, if you like I'll assess Michael's condition.

COMMENTS ON CASE 2

The preceding interview represents the initial contracting with the client—in this case, two clients. Although the purpose of the work is still vague, the worker and Carla have some direction for their respective tasks or activities. Carla wants the worker for one purpose—that is, to tell her if there is any hope for her husband and if so, how he can be helped. Her perception of the situation represents the presenting problem, as is the case with any client in any initial social work encounter. The worker, who is a solo practitioner, and whose work therefore is not guided by any agency function, must identify a role for herself (let's assume this worker is a woman)—a role that suits her ideological orientation and technical capabilities. This worker's role is informed by the generic psychiatric social work principles outlined above. The contract will serve in the place of the agency function in defining the scope and limits of her work with Carla and Michael. Diagnosis will be related to the use of particular gerontological social work services, ranging from comprehensive assessment and problem solving interventions to coordination of resources and collaboration with other professionals. The worker's intention is not to change the character of either client, but rather, to help the clients get over various obstacles to their effective functioning. Yet the worker must be diagnostically astute, or the clients will suffer the consequences of an inadequate helping strategy.

DIFFERENTIAL DIAGNOSIS

In the course of working with the couple in case 2, two central themes emerged: Carla's obstinacy was a fixed and mixed blessing, and Michael's diagnosis continued to be a puzzle.

Carla's obstinacy helped to keep the work on target, through her constant inquiries regarding the progress (or lack thereof) of the helping engagement. In addition, however, her stubbornness seemed to be rooted in denial of her own motives, needs, and feelings. As the work progressed, Carla began to use the sessions to air her own frustrations and issues related to the demands of caregiving; but she failed to see this as any valid reason for the sessions. The worker chose to collude with Carla in denying her neediness for the sake of helping her to cope with the difficulties of caring for her husband. Instead of confronting Carla with her resistance to her own needs, the worker agreed to define the "real" giving of help as being related to attempts to heighten Michael's alertness and functioning. Insofar as this was concerned, the worker used the technique known as life review or reminiscence as a way to enlist the long term memory of an individual who was experiencing deficits in short term memory. This technique helps people to use what they have left and connect with another person in a nonthreatening interaction. All the while—in the initial phases of work—the worker attempted to obtain data that would shed light on the meaning of Michael's symptoms.

Differential diagnosis is the process by which symptoms are separated into diagnostic categories for the purpose of distinguishing one syndrome of morbidity from another. It is common knowledge that depression can be confused with dementia, and that some dementias are reversible and therefore are not really dementias at all but states of delirium. Symptoms may overlap—a person who is in the early stages of Alzheimer's disease will most certainly be depressed; and depressed individuals often seem disconnected or detached from reality. Michael's behavior was contradictory. At times he seemed totally withdrawn—but at other times he was extremely lucid, even witty. His mental status did *not* show the classic feature of Alzheimer's disease: consistent degeneration. That is, he didn't seem to get worse. This prompted the social worker to send him to a geriatrician for further evaluation. The geriatrician believed that Michael's depressed cognitive functioning might be associated with electroshock treatments that he had received when he was first diagnosed with depression, shortly after his retirement. The psychiatrist was then called on to reevaluate Michael and placed him on a new antidepressant, which seemed to calm him and reduce the agitation that went along with his social withdrawal. The geriatrician also diagnosed a bladder problem which needed to be surgically corrected (bladder stones). The surgery was successful, but Michael's mental condition took a sharp turn for the worse. Ultimately, he was rehospitalized and given a complete diagnostic workup, including a brain CT scan. The scan revealed a brain tumor. Michael died within 1 month of this last hospitalization. The preceding events had taken place over 6 months. Case 2 is presented to illustrate the importance of differential diagnosis and comprehensive physical, medical, and psychological assessment. Were Michael's earlier symptoms related to the existence of the tumor? Why did the doctors who originally treated him for depression not send him for a CT scan when his depression was not lifted by medication or electroshock treatments? Why were they so quick to label Michael as having Alzheimer's disease?

QUESTIONS FOR DISCUSSION: DIFFERENTIAL DIAGNOSIS IN CASE 2

1. Who is the client in case 2?
2. If Michael is the client, what is the worker's role with Carla?
3. If the couple is viewed as the client, how does that affect the work?
4. Why is comprehensive assessment particularly important in the case of an older individual?
5. What is the importance of appropriate collaboration in a situation such as that of Michael and Carla?
6. In offering Michael and Carla comprehensive service, what professionals would you include in your collaborative network?
7. What skills did the worker use in the first conversation with Carla?
8. What fundamental task was the worker addressing in the first interview with Carla?
9. How might the worker's status as a solo practitioner affect the work?
10. What might characterize the nature of the worker's continuing work with Carla? What would be the focus?

THE MEANING OF RELATIONSHIP

The concept of *relationship* is used differently in different theoretical frameworks. Variations in theoretical orientation reflect varying interpretations regarding the centrality of the worker-client relationship to the helping process. Also reflected are varying interpretations regarding the connection between the relationship and the purpose of the work.

In Smalley's concept, the relationship is viewed as central to the helping process, but limits are placed on the use of the relationship. Just as diagnosis is related to function or specific purpose, the relationship between the worker and the client is limited by the specific purpose of the work. Worker–client interaction focuses on the work. Interpretation of the client's character and conflicts is limited to the relevance of this understanding to task performance. This keeps the work on target.

The significance of the contributions of the early functionalists to modern developments in psychoanalytic treatment methodology cannot be overstated. Although there was a parting of the ways between the proponents of the diagnostic and functional approaches, modern developments in object relations theory, ego psychology, and psychoanalytic treatment are based on two fundamental principles of functionalism: (1) the importance of setting limits in defining a purpose for the work; and (2) the centrality of the nature of the interaction between the client and the worker to the client's movement in the process (Greenberg & Mitchell, 1983). Although it is beyond the scope of this book to analyze the relative meaning of the concepts of diagnosis, relationship and purpose in psychoanalytic theory, functionalism provides an elegant formulation of the correlation among these concepts which is worthy of scholarly reflection. Pioneers in the development of functionalism deserve praise for their insight, and (in retrospect) for their foresight. The gerontological social work practitioner who works in the field of mental health benefits from advanced clinical training in diagnosis and communication, as well as the skillful handling of transference and resistance. All of these concepts can be integrated within a functional orientation based on Smalley's principles of diagnosis, relationship, and the agency's purpose.

The relationship between worker and client develops in the process of addressing and completing a task. The relationship develops through communication between worker and client. According to Shulman (1992), "The relationship is not separate from the work, but rather it is part of the work."

Shulman goes on to say: "The ability of the worker to be tuned in to the unspoken feelings and concerns of the client in the preliminary phase of work, and then to articulate these feelings, contributes to the establishment of a positive working relationship" (p. 60). Shulman defines the connection between feelings and actions. The worker's role is described as being guided by the principle of helping the client *deal with feelings in pursuit of purpose* (p. 23). These principles clearly relate to the generic principles we outlined here. Transference and resistance are not ignored. They represent existential processes that are dealt with by the worker as they promote or impede the progress of the work as defined by the contract.

The worker uses various communication methods to deal with the performance of the work and other communication methods to deal with helping clients manage their feelings, or the affective tone of the work. Methods of communication are elaborated in Chapter 11.

The importance of establishing a positive working relationship is not restricted to casework. Building relationships is equally important in working with small and even large groups. The worker must also be attuned to the thoughts and feelings of all members of the client system if he or she is to be effective in pursuing the purpose of the work.

THE FAMILY:
IMPLICATIONS FOR THE HELPING PROCESS

The concept of family, too, is understood differently in different practice orientations. In family practice, the family is viewed as the client and strategies for intervention are aimed at improving family dynamics. In gerontological social work practice, although the family often is relevant to the helping process, our formulation identifies the older person as the client. This understanding protects the older person from becoming the victim of a helping strategy that is being promoted for the benefit of the whole family, and it reduces the risk of jeopardizing the older person's self-interest. Sometimes the interests of all family members can be balanced in identifying helping objectives. However, in the event of a conflict of interest, each party should have the advantage of independent psychosocial counseling and assistance.

In chapter 4, we have demonstrated the application of an integrative methodology to gerontological psychiatric social work practice, or to work with older clients in mental health settings. The case examples illustrate the generic principles of comprehensive biopsychosocial assessment, the importance of a specific purpose, the connection between diagnosis and function, the connection between relationship and use of service, and the importance of developing collaborative contacts with families and with other professionals. These principles are the same in any field of service delivery. The purpose of the work or the contract is what distinguishes work in the various social settings. In the mental health setting, the social worker requires advanced knowledge of psychosocial assessment and mental disease. The purpose of the work, which is defined in relation to specific tasks, determines the application of this specialized knowledge. The agency's function and the contract between worker and client define the particular tasks that are addressed. In all other respects, work with the client in the mental health setting is no different from work with clients in other settings.

REFERENCES

Blanck, G., & Blanck, R, (1974). *Ego psychology: Theory and practice.* New York: Columbia University Press.

Greenberg, J.R., & Mitchell,S.A. (1983). *Object relations in psychoanalytic theory.* Cambridge, MA: Harvard University Press.

Shulman, L. (1992). *The skills of helping.* Itasca, IL: Peacock.

Schwartz, W., & Zalba, S. (1971) *The practice of group work.* New York: Columbia University Press.

Tirrito, T., Nathanson, I., & Langer, N. (1996). *Elder practice: A multidisciplinary approach to working with older adults in the community.* Columbia, SC: University of South Carolina Press.

CHAPTER 5

Formal Social Services

INTRODUCTION

The passage of the Older Americans Act (1965) provided an impetus for the establishment of formal social services for older people. In addition to providing funding for a number of services—including Meals-on-Wheels, information and referral services, telephone reassurance, senior centers, and more recently the Ombudsman program (an advocacy program designed for the protection of nursing home residents)—the act established an organizational framework for the delivery of these services under the authority of the Federal Administration on Aging. Local or area agencies for aging were established to coordinate services on a regional level. Area agencies for aging—called triple-A agencies—are responsible for supervising the delivery of services under the Older Americans Act. It has become common practice for the government to contract out some services to voluntary agencies that serve older adults in the community. Therefore, the area agencies for aging are charged with the additional responsibility of coordinating these public-private partnerships.

The formal system of social services delivery is fragmented and in reality is a composite of three separate systems: the aging services system; the social services system, and the health system. There is much overlap in terms of the types of programs provided under the auspices of each. For example, case management services are provided by hospitals and community health agencies, by older adult counseling services, by meal programs,

44

by recreational programs, and by local departments of social services. To reduce this overlap and create greater efficiency, there has been some effort to coordinate the application processes and service delivery activities of programs provided under different public rubrics. These efforts have had some success, for example, through adopting common screening tools and providing a single point of entry into the system or systems for older people.

The gerontological social worker in any aspect of elder practice (e.g., health, mental health, legal, or political) must be familiar with the total spectrum of formal social, health, and legal services. However, the gerontological social worker in a formal social service agency has the privilege and responsibility of being a member of the host profession in these agencies. In other words, the gerontological social worker in aging services is well positioned for political influence since the formal mission of these agencies is to serve older people in the community. The worker has the force of the agency behind him or her.

THE ROLE OF THE GERONTOLOGICAL SOCIAL WORKER IN DELIVERY OF FORMAL SOCIAL SERVICES

The great advantage of working for a social service agency is that the role of the social worker is strongly supported by the institution in which it is embedded. The social worker in services to the aging is a specialist in the delivery of social and health services for older people. The job requires comprehensive knowledge of the needs of older people, and of the agencies and individuals that provide formal social and health services to them. Case management function is high among the tasks of gerontological social workers in formal social services delivery. Equally important are diagnostic knowledge, the use of relationships in diagnosis and in giving help, and knowledge and skill in collaborative techniques and strategic planning. The role is multifaceted and yet specifically defined by the focus of the particular gerontological service being delivered.

The social worker's role in delivery of formal social services may involve all of the different methods—ranging from the primary methods of casework, group work, and community organization to the secondary administrative and supervisory methods. In Smalley's concept, the generic principles that underlie all of these methods are the same. Each relies on the agency's purpose and the relationship with the client or the client group as being fundamental to assessment of needs or diagnosis and to movement in the process. One can look on the work of the gerontological social worker in this area as the consummate role, because of the opportunities for using the various methods of social work and for influencing organizational purposes. There is a saying that "one can be only as honest as the system will allow." What greater opportunity for scrupulous professional behavior than within a system whose very framework derives from professional principles?

CASE EXAMPLE: AN OLDER APPLICANT FOR MEALS-ON-WHEELS

The case example presented below illustrates the complexity of being a gerontological social worker in delivery of services to aging people. The case examines the application process in an older man's request for Meals-on-Wheels, a home meal delivery program for people in need. The case illustrates the importance of comprehensive screening, collaboration among professionals, and the "institutionalization" of integrated approaches to service delivery. The case also illustrates the resistance of many older people to receiving what they may regard as "welfare."

> Walter Thompson is a 78-year-old Black man who lives alone with his seeing-eye dog, Scout. Mr. Thompson has a number of chronic conditions including hypertension, diabetes, and blindness from glaucoma. He has been blind for the last 6 years but has managed his own personal care, and he gets around with the assistance of his dog. He attends social programs at a local agency that serves the visually impaired, but at the point when this case begins he hadn't been attending for many weeks because of inclement weather.

> The social worker at the agency was concerned about Mr. Thompson and called to find out how he was managing. Before this absence he had been receiving his midday meal routinely at the agency, under a joint venture arrangement with the local senior center. Under this arrangement a percentage of federal lunch funds are shared to ensure that older adults with visual impairments have the same meal privilege as regular senior center members.

> Mr. Thompson is a retired airplane mechanic who worked for a cargo transport company. He receives Social Security, amounting to $693 per month. He pays $250 per month to rent a one-room efficiency apartment in a private home. The cost of his telephone and utilities comes to an additional $65 per month. He is left with just enough money to meet his monthly living expenses, including, food, clothes, and sundries. He re-

ceives Medicare and participates in EPIC, a government prescription program which relieves him of most of the cost of his medications. Mr. Thompson is divorced. He has two sons. One of his sons is in the armed services and is stationed oversees. He hears from this son occasionally; but has little contact with the other son, who lives in the same town with his own family and his mother, Mr. Thompson's ex-wife.

After the call to Mr. Thompson, the social worker contacted the senior center to find out if there was any way he might be eligible for Meals-on-Wheels. She was told to contact the Meals-on-Wheels office, which operates out of the basement of a Baptist church. She arranged for the social worker from Meals-on-Wheels to make a home visit to Mr. Thompson. The social worker at the agency for the visually impaired thought that Mr. Thompson should be reevaluated regarding the scope of his need for services, and the Meals-on-Wheels worker said that would be part of the assessment. The following interview represents the exchange between the worker and Mr. Thompson.

INTERVIEW

Worker: Thank you for letting me in, Mr. Thompson. (Takes his hand in greeting), My name is Hank Crosby. I'm a social worker with Meals-on-Wheels.

Walter: My name's Walter; please call me that. Say hello to Scout.

Worker: Hi, Scout. You seem to be managing pretty well, but I imagine it has been hard for you, not being able to get out.

Walter: This snow has been bad for Scout and me, but we manage—don't we, boy. The man who owns the house walks him for me.

Worker: I can see Scout is very important to you.

Walter: He is my best friend. Truly, I would not have been able to survive these past years without Scout.

Worker: The glaucoma?

Walter: Let me tell you, young man, I was a fool not to take care of my eyes....Funny, though, I seem to see things clearer, now that I'm blind.

Worker: What things are clearer?

Walter: Too many things to waste your time with....I hear you may be able to have a meal delivered here. That would be real nice, until I can get out again.

Worker: Do you mind answering some questions? I got a lot of information from Leslie at the Center, but I just need to get a little bit more.

Walter: I'm glad to have you here. You don't have to hesitate to ask anything.

Worker: Thank you. I'm curious to know where you get your medical care.

Walter: I go to the medical clinic at St. Joseph's. I see Dr. Perry for my high blood pressure, and I sometimes see Dr. Fernandez—he's a vascular specialist—for complications from my diabetes.

Worker: When was the last time you were examined?

Walter: About 3 months ago. I have to go for the medication refills. I take inderal, oral insulin (oral hypoglycemic medication) and aspirin.

Worker: You seem to stay on top of your health?

Walter: Now. I should have done it years ago, before I made a mess of myself.

Worker: How do you see that you made a mess?

Walter: I thought you came about a meal program.

Worker: Maybe I should have been clearer. I came to give you a full evaluation to see how you're managing....and to see if there's anything in addition to the meals that might be helpful to you.

Walter: I could use some good weather. (Laughs.)

Worker: I didn't say I could perform a miracle, did I? (Both laugh.)

Walter: Well, I am a little worried about this weather, and you know, I'm not a total fool....I know my diabetes is getting worse, because I have trouble with swelling in my left foot. I should be seeing the doctor; but it's not bad enough to call an ambulance.

Worker: What about home care? Doesn't St. Joe's have a home care department?

Walter: I never inquired.

Worker: You know, Walter, you may be entitled to a lot more benefits if you had Medicaid. Medicaid pays for a lot more home services than Medicare.

Walter: What do you have to do to qualify?

Worker: You have to turn in some financial information to the Medicaid office or, maybe, there's a Medicaid representative at the hospital. We can check it out.

Walter: Is that like welfare? Because if it is, I don't want anything to do with it.

Worker: It's a program run by Social Services. What's wrong with that?

Walter: I haven't been the best of men, but I ain't the worst. I always supported myself...never took any handouts. When Agnes and I split up, I always saw to it that she got a good part of my income for herself and the boys. I'm not a bum, whatever it might look like now.

Worker: I wouldn't have assumed you were a bum, as you put it. What would make you feel that way?

Walter: There you go again, asking too many questions. Are you some kind of a psychiatrist?

Worker: And what does that mean to you, Mr. Thompson? (Good-humoredly)

Walter: I guess I should be appreciating your interest, instead of giving you a hard time. It's just that I guess I'm not used to having visitors.

Worker: Especially one who seems to ask prying questions.... but really, Walter, what are you being so hard on yourself for? You've said you've been a fool—Something is obviously bothering you.

Walter: I'd just like to make some peace with my family before I die, maybe even make peace with myself. I can't say I've been suffering these last years since I lost my sight….but that's because of Scout….Things could get worse.

Worker: You could get needier.

Walter: That's part of what eats at me. Did I deserve this?

Worker: Do you think you deserve to be blind?

Walter: Everything happens for a reason, young man—that's what I think.

Worker: Maybe so. Do you think we could talk again, Walter? I could come back next week to see how you are enjoying the meals.

Walter: You mean I'll be getting the lunches?

Worker: Isn't that why I came to see you? You don't think I'd hold back on that after bothering you with all these questions, do you?

QUESTIONS FOR DISCUSSION: THE INTERVIEW

1. What would be important to know about Walter's medical conditions? What is the possible relationship between the high blood pressure and the diabetes?

2. Did the worker make the purpose of the interview clear enough at the beginning of the interview?

3. How does Walter's resistance manifest itself?

4. Are Walter's conflicts internal, external, or both?

5. Is it important that this worker understand the nature of Walter's conflicts?

6. Did the worker handle Walter's resistance properly? How might it have been handled differently?

7. What might be the worker's continuing strategy for working with Walter? What tasks might the worker address with Walter?

8. What would be the appropriate role for the worker in coordinating services for Walter?

9. What additional information would be essential in assessing the full scope of Walter's biopsychosocial needs?

10. Would you suggest that Walter's family be included in the needs assessment? If so, how would you go about assessing the possible role of the family in the management of Walter's continued care?

COMPREHENSIVE ASSESSMENT

One significant aspect of working with older people is the importance of providing a comprehensive assessment of their medical, psychological, and social needs. There is an interrelationship among all of these factors, and a weakness in one area of functioning will have ramifications for other areas of functioning.

In the case example, Walter seems to be carrying a burden of unresolved family conflicts and issues of self-esteem. These issues may increase his fear of being isolated as his caregiving needs escalate, and that in turn could create greater stress for his physical condition and result in increased hypertension. If his diabetes is not monitored closely, secondary atherosclerosis can also adversely influence his circulation and blood pressure. The oral hypoglycemic medication may not be sufficient, and if he needs insulin, someone would have to inject the insulin on a daily basis. This might create the need for home care but without Medicaid, there is no way that Walter is going to be able to pay for this service. If Walter had Medicaid in place he could breathe a little more freely, knowing that he was prepared for this eventuality. Sometimes people think that they deserve their fate, and overcoming Walter's resistance to helping himself may become an important focus of the worker's task. But where does the worker begin?

Smalley's framework provides a guide. The worker must come to the next session with Walter with a clear understanding of the purpose of their activity together. The worker's definition of the task flows from a comprehensive assessment of the client's needs, as well as from the agency's purpose. Therefore, more information regarding the scope of these needs may be necessary. The worker's continuing diagnosis of Walter's psychosocial condition will take place in the context of their mutually agreed upon goals for the client. These goals are directly affected by the purpose of the agency. In other words, if Walter needs help with filing a Medicaid application and help negotiating his relationship with his family, the worker needs to evaluate whether these tasks are appropriate aspects of his role. Should the worker at the agency for the visually impaired be the one to make the contact with the family?

Who is going to assist Walter with the Medicaid application? This is where the worker must draw on his skill in coordinating activities among providers. Often, a worker will find that there are many areas of overlap in the definition of the roles of different service providers, and this overlap creates confusion. An astute worker will try to clarify the activities of the different providers to avoid overlap and to facilitate delivery of services. On the other hand, sometimes no one claims authority for a particular function. For example, the Medicaid office may require that Walter appear in person at the office. Who is going to take Walter to the Medicaid office? Proficient workers recognize when there is a gap in coordination. They will attempt to make a change in the formal system by instituting a general mechanism for handling this type of situation. A change in the formal system ensures that the job is not handled idiosyncratically. Provision has been made for future incidents of this type.

CASE SUPERVISORY MEETING

The following interview represents the discussion the worker ("Hank") has with his supervisor ("Sup") at the Meals-on-Wheels site regarding the matter of the Medicaid application process.

Hank:	I'm not really sure what areas are appropriate for me to get involved with in Mr. Thompson's case. He needs a lot of services besides the meals.
Sup:	What part are you unsure of?
Hank:	Well, he seems to need help with his family. I spoke with the social worker at the agency for the visually impaired, and the social worker thought she should handle that because of her relationship with Walter. Also, they're equipped there to do short-term counseling. They have psychiatric backup. The area I'm having a problem with is Medicaid. Walter needs someone to go with him to the Medicaid office, but that's going to be an all-day affair, at least. I called the Medicaid office and they said they don't provide home visits.
Sup:	Whom did you speak with?
Hank:	One of the supervisors there. She said they don't have the staff to send out. I think they should have that service. You know, I could take Walter, but I really don't think it should be our role. Who is supposed to be handling the case management for our clients?
Sup:	That's a good question. Generally, we work it out with the referring agency on a case-by-case basis. It usually works out, but we've always had a problem with these Medicaid applications for our homebound clients. Fortunately, Mr. Thompson can get out.
Hank:	Are you saying I should take him over.... It's okay with me.
Sup:	Maybe,... but first check with Sister Susan. She usually comes up with a volunteer or does it herself if necessary.
Hank:	I hate to go to her. She's already overworked.
Sup:	I know. I'm having a meeting with the commissioner on Wednesday. I'm going to bring this issue up. Maybe she can work something out with Social Services on a formal level. It's getting to be a real problem with these homebound clients. So many can't get out. It's a real Catch 22.

Hank: I'm curious to know how far I'm expected to get involved with our clients. So many of them seem to be falling through the cracks.

Sup: There's no cut-and-dried answer to that question. I go to the Inter-Agency Council meetings and we try to work out some of the snags in the case management.... maybe you should come. One of the biggest problems we have in this agency is with referrals from either private doctors or family members. Most of those clients don't have a clue about entitlements or benefits or what they should be doing to plan for incapacity. If it's any help, you have to be guided by our general procedures. After the person is on the meal program, you visit only in an emergency. In other words, the general case management is provided through Community Support Services. If you think this man is going to need ongoing counseling, I'd bring them on board.... Call the Area Agency, and they'll hook you up with someone.

Hank: I just don't want to see this man tossed around from agency to agency.

Sup: Why don't you continue to see him weekly until you've made the transition?

Hank: That sounds fair.

This meeting illustrates the agency's role in determining the function of the worker and the great amount of work that goes into clarification of roles and strategic planning. The planning activities extend to the macro-organizational level, as evidenced by the supervisor's function in developing policy.

COLLABORATION

With regard to collaboration, we elaborate the concepts in our earlier book (Tirrito, Nathanson, & Langer, 1996).

KEY PRINCIPLES

It is appropriate to delineate some key principles of the multidisciplinary approach to the provision of formal services to an older population.

1. *Know the scope and limits of one's responsibility.* It is important to clarify one's own tasks and the limitations of one's own activities, as this gives sharp focus to one's activities and avoids overlap.

2. *Access other disciplines.* The key to forming effective links with other providers is getting to know the community agencies and practitioners

in the area and establishing agreements about the scope and limits of each other's involvement.

3. *Maintain consistent contact with other professionals.* This requires informal meetings as well as participation in interagency councils. Many disciplines are involved in the provision of services to the elderly, including medical doctors, dentists, lawyers, religious leaders, nurses, and social workers. Some of these professionals are self-employed; some are agency-based. Gerontological social workers must know their clients' service system—in all its individual and peculiar aspects—in order to know where to begin forging collaborative links.

SPECIFIC STRATEGIES FOR PROMOTING COLLABORATION

1. Establish a consensus with other professionals regarding the purpose of the collaboration.
2. Define the nature of each other's professional tasks.
3. Establish an agreement regarding preferred outcomes for elderly clients or patients.

OBSTACLES TO COLLABORATION

1. Failure to establish consensus regarding the reason for the collaboration and the objectives for the collaboration.
2. Territoriality among different service providers who want to control the case management process.
3. Family dynamics that are disruptive to cooperative activities.
4. Crisis situations that require immediate solutions and create stress for professionals.

The impact of these obstacles can be avoided or reduced by recognizing that they are sometimes inevitable, by planning for them and by focusing efforts early on resolving conflicts and potential problems in continuity of care management.

CULTURAL INFLUENCES

We would be seriously remiss if we did not explore the cultural aspects of this case as well as the broader implications of ethnogerontology. *Ethnogerontology* is "the study of the causes, processes, and consequences of race, national origin and culture on individual and population aging" (Hooyman & Kiyak, 1993, p. 443). Ethnicity may be discussed as involving three components: "a culture and an internalized common heritage which are not fully understood or shared by outsiders; social status; and support systems (Barresi & Skull, in Hooyman and Kiyak, 1993, p. 441). Ethnicity may or may not encompass minority status, although minority status is represented in our case example.

Minority status and gender are two factors that typically exacerbate the vulnerability of the aging individual to financial and social insecurities. Therefore, ethnic minority people are exposed to a type of "double jeopardy." Ethnic minority status affects one's financial condition, insofar as lifetime employment is linked with ethnicity in the United States. Ethnic minorities are less likely than their white counterparts to have an uninterrupted work history—the kind of work history that is associated with pensions and maximum Social Security benefits in retirement. The medical and social picture is a bit more complicated than the financial picture. Black men who reach age 80 and over are likely to be in better health than their White counterparts, since a higher percentage of Black males than White males die before this age as a result of lifestyle and environmental hazards (accidents) (Hooyman & Kiyak, 1993). In our case example, Mr. Thompson's financial status and medical status both reflect the hazards of his work and health histories (e.g., no pension and no preventive eye care.) These factors can be linked to his social status. In addition, although Mr. Thompson has a good formal social system operating to his advantage, he has little or no connection to any family or informal support. Black American women typically have more extended family involvement than their White counterparts, and Black married men benefit from these connections; however, Mr. Thompson's divorce seems to have isolated him from his family. This feature of his experience is unfortunately characteristic of many divorced men of all races in this country and may be related more to gender than ethnicity.

It is part of the worker's responsibility to understand the impact of all these cultural factors in forming a comprehensive assessment of a client's situation. One can see from Mr. Thompson's remark, "I'm not a bum," that he is defensive. Perhaps he is ashamed and guilty about some aspect of his past. He may also be concerned about how a White worker (let's assume that this worker is White) may be viewing him and may want to feel that he is not being judged by an outsider who doesn't understand. We can also learn something from Mr. Thompson's language. Is he communicating more formally than he might be if he were speaking to a Black worker? If his resistance can't be overcome, would it not be preferable to have a new, Black worker assigned to the case? This underscores the importance of having a diversified staff. All of these factors affect the assessment and the ongoing work with the client. Of no less importance is an understanding of the significance of extended family ties within the Black community. Would a Black family that appreciates extended family ties be receptive to providing some assistance to an estranged father?

Understanding cultural influences, then, is critical to social work practice with older people, and this includes understanding the impact of gender and sexual orientation on the experience of aging, particularly as these factors relate to social status and existing support systems.

On a macro level, the worker must also address the social inequalities which make aging individuals vulnerable. This requires certain programmatic and planning expertise (which will explored further in Chapter 10). Since the agency's purpose represents the connection between the community interest and the worker's role or function with each client or client group, the worker has a responsibility to mediate between the needs of his or her clients and the purposes of the various systems (including the agency) in which they are engaged.

The case of Walter Thompson illustrates the necessity of comprehensive assessment and micro, or casework, planning. It also illustrates the importance of specificity of function not only in facilitating the goals of the client, but in defining and clarifying the goals of the various agencies and individuals that constitute the formal system or systems of services. Skill in collaboration is essential in meeting the established goals. Specificity of function is also critically related to relationship and diagnosis. The relationship between worker and client develops in relation to an agreed-upon purpose. The relationship informs the worker's understanding of the client's personality structure, object relations, defenses, and conflicts. These aspects of character are evaluated in relation to the work, as they facilitate or impede the work's progress. The limits focus the energies of worker and client on a common goal and help to avoid random activity. These are generic principles that derive from the functional perspective as outlined by Smalley and elaborated by us.

REFERENCES

Hooyman, N., & Kiyak, A.H. (1993). *Social gerontology* (3rd ed.). Boston: Allyn and Bacon.

Tirrito, T., Nathanson, I., & Langer, N. (1996) *Elder practice: a multidisciplinary approach to working with older adults in the community.* Columbia, SC: University of South Carolina Press.

CHAPTER 6

Gerontological Social Work Practice in Health Services

INTRODUCTION

Social workers practice in a variety of health care settings. They work in agencies or solo private practices. Several states regulate social work services in health care settings such as nursing homes, home care agencies, hospices, and hospitals. Gerontological social workers practice in hospitals, nursing homes, rehabilitation centers, day care centers, home health care agencies, hospices, and even physicians' offices. Gerontological social workers can be solo private practitioners such as geriatric psychotherapists or geriatric consultants to psychiatrists, geriatricians, psychologists, nursing homes, and home health care agencies. In a health care environment, gerontological social work practice is a multidisciplinary activity in which social work is often ancillary to the medical treatment team. The social worker's tasks include counseling, discharge planning, resource acquisition, family assessment, advocacy, and interdisciplinary planning.

This chapter examines gerontological social work practice in a specialized setting: health services. We will discuss three settings: nursing homes, home health care agencies, and acute care hospitals. Although there are other health care settings in which social workers practice (such as hospices, rehabilitation centers, physicians' offices, and dialysis centers) we have chosen these three specific settings to illustrate gerontological social work practice because the population in these settings is predominately older.

In a health care setting, the social worker is a member of a multidisciplinary team but has very different responsibilities from the other team members. While the responsibilities of medical social work vary in different states, the social worker's role is always an essential one in a health care environment. Gerontology is recognized as a multidisciplinary activity, and health care for older adults is approached from a multidisciplinary perspective (Ferraro, 1990). Thus the gerontological social worker in a health care environment has a unique role as a member of the multidisciplinary team. As a professional whose training includes a holistic approach to assessment, treatment and intervention, the gerontological social worker has a biopsychosocial orientation. The biopsychosocial factors that impact the client's medical condition are assessed in diagnosis and treatment. A team approach is used to develop a multidisciplinary plan for the patient, outlining specific goals and objectives to be accomplished by professionals from the various disciplines. The multidisciplinary team approach avoids duplication of services and, most important, promotes communication among professionals that results in a sharing of knowledge and expertise. The acceptance of a multidisciplinary approach to solving problems is what distinguishes gerontological social work practice in this setting from social work practice in other settings.

SOCIAL WORK PRACTICE IN A NURSING HOME

What is social work practice in a nursing home? In nursing homes, social workers are involved with the client from admission to discharge. The social worker conducts a psychosocial assessment, counsels the client and family, develops a care plan with other team members, acts as the client's advocate to obtain services from community agencies, and may even train the staff in psychosocial issues of institutionalized and frail older adults. Social workers in nursing homes are also frequently responsible for training the staff regarding patients' rights (Hancock, 1990). Social workers help the client to navigate in this environment (e.g., clients often develop "learned helplessness" in an institutional, paternalistic environment). Clients' right to choose and refuse health care and treatment can cause conflict between patients and staff, and social workers are often called to mediate in such conflict.

The social worker's primary task in a nursing home, however, is to help the client, now considered a patient, to adjust to "institutionalization." Although many nursing homes make a valiant effort to create a homelike atmosphere, nursing homes are not "homes." Nursing homes in our society are medical facilities based on a medical treatment model. Adjustment to life in a nursing home means adapting to routines, to schedules, and to being dependent on the staff for treatment and services. Older persons are adaptable and adjust to many of life's situations, but the combination of loss of health, dependence on others for care, and change in living environment requires a great deal of adjustment. Social workers play a pivotal role in this adjustment process by counseling and offering support.

Social workers are also discharge planners and often arrange for alternative placement in other types of living facilities, with family members, or in another nursing home. Often when a patient is discharged home, the social worker arranges for home-delivered meals, a housekeeper, or a physical therapist to provide assistance with activities of daily living. If financial help is needed, the social worker applies to Medicaid or Supplementary Security Income for assistance.

Social work practice in a nursing home, then, involves mediation, advocacy, training, counseling, planning, and resource allocation. In addition, the social worker must have specialized knowledge of medical procedures, medications, and nursing care.

SOCIAL WORK PRACTICE IN A
HOME HEALTH CARE AGENCY

Social work practice in home health care agencies is growing rapidly as community services become the focal point for care of older persons. Social workers in home health care agencies are members of a multidisciplinary team of nurses, physicians, physical therapists, nutritionists, and psychologists. When patients are discharged from a hospital they may be referred to home health care agencies that monitor their progress and provide nursing treatments such as injections for diabetics or changes of surgical dressings. The patient's physician is the primary referral person for home care services, which often include the services not only of a nurse but also of a physical therapist and a social worker.

The social worker's task is to assess the client's psychosocial needs, provide counseling, and link the client or family to community agencies for additional services such as Meals-on-Wheels and housekeeping. A primary task for the social worker is the psychosocial assessment. It must be comprehensive and include the biopsychosocial factors affecting the client's medical condition. For example, is the home environment hindering the client's recovery? Who are the caregivers, if any? What are the client's financial resources? Does the client have enough money for medication?

What is the client's emotional state? Is the client cognitively intact? Is the client showing signs of depression? What community services does the client need? The social worker completes the assessment and recommends additional services for the client. The multidisciplinary team (nurse, social worker, nutritionist, physical therapist) develops goals and objectives for the patient in a collaborative effort with the patient's physician.

Home visits are the province of social work and provide the opportunity for the social worker to make an assessment in the client's environment. The social worker is able to determine the psychobehavioral status of the patient or client. Some questions are: Does the client express any particular problems? Does the client seem to have adequate or inadequate coping skills? Is the client disoriented or confused? Is the client able to leave home? Can the client leave home without assistance? Is the client primarily homebound?

The services of a home health care agency are generally intended as a short-term intervention after discharge from a hospital. Thus social work intervention is brief in home health care situations. The social work tasks are primarily assessment, counseling, referral, advocacy, and collaboration.

SOCIAL WORK PRACTICE IN AN ACUTE CARE HOSPITAL

Social work practice in an acute care hospital is usually referred to as medical social work practice. Medical social workers have large caseloads which include older adults since the number of hospitals that have increased their long term care beds has grown significantly (Hooyman & Kiyak, 1996). Medical social work practice includes counseling patients and families, arranging for home care services, and applying for financial assistance. In gerontological medical social work practice, the social worker is assigned specifically to older adults or to a geriatric unit in the hospital.

Social work departments in hospitals can be independent units or discharge planning units in a utilization review department. Discharge planning has been a major responsibility for hospital social workers since 1983 when diagnostic related groups (DRGs) were implemented. After the implementation of DRGs, the acute care hospital became more concerned with costs of care. Under this prospective payment system, Medicare limits reimbursement for "patient care days" according to the patient's diagnosis, and discharge planning involves moving the patient out of the hospital prior to the termination of reimbursement. Discharge planning involves planning appropriate continuing care for the patient. The patient is discharged to a rehabilitation facility, a nursing home, a retirement home, a hospice, a private home, or an "assisted living" apartment. When professional community help is needed, referrals are made to a home health care agency. Coordinating community services involves sifting through the criteria for home services reimbursed by Medicare or Medicaid. In these cases, the social worker may serve as advocate in securing appropriate benefits (Hancock, 1990).

The medical social worker counsels older adults in hospitals to explore alternative medical procedures and treatments and to cope with functional limitations after an illness. Social work practice includes mental health screening for indicators of depression, alcoholism, or of suicide. Hospital social workers also act as advocates in what is often a paternalistic environment. Paternalistic attitudes reflect an attempt to protect the frail older adult, and social workers frequently must act as advocates for the patient's right to self-determination. Ageist attitudes equate physical frailty with mental incompetence, and hospital social workers play a pivotal role as advocates for a client's right to choose and to refuse treatments. Ethical decisions create conflict among patients, family members, and health care professionals. Social workers may mediate in this process. Refusal to use or refusal to withdraw life-sustaining equipment or feeding tubes is an area of potential conflict (Moody, 1994). Autonomy in decision making and the right to self-determination are two fundamental values of social work. They are integral to medical social work practice but often must be balanced against the older person's need for protection. This can create an ethical conflict for the social worker which also must be resolved.

PRINCIPLES

The six principles applied throughout this book are a conceptual framework for gerontological social work practice. These six principles for gerontological social work practice are derived from generic social work principles proposed by Smalley. We believe that these principles are universally applied by social workers in all settings and with all age groups, but the specialized knowledge needed for working with older adults demands an understanding that is specific to gerontological social work practice. The application of this integrative methodology is illustrated in the case examples.

The six principles are:

  I.   Diagnosis or assessment of need
 II.   Agency function
III.   Use of service

IV.   Use of administrative skills
V.   Use of relationship
VI.   Use of collaboration

How do these principles apply in a health care setting? First, comprehensive diagnosis of the older adult in a health care setting must not focus primarily on the client's pathology. It must include the client's mental status, spiritual needs, and legal, financial, and social condition. Understanding of the client's physical condition is most effective when the client's physical condition is placed in context with the client's other needs. Second, the function of the agency—hospital, nursing home, or home care agency—gives direction and focus to the work, and social work tasks differ in each of these three settings as required by the agency. Third, the client's relationship with the social worker is of central importance in a health care setting because of the particular vulnerability of clients who are faced with life-and-death decisions. Trust in the relationship between worker and client is crucial in working through some of these life crisis decisions. Fourth, use of collaboration is essential in a health care setting because of the comprehensive needs of clients and patients in the multidisciplinary organizational structure. The remaining two principles—use of service and administrative skills—probably need no elaboration here.

THE WORKER'S ROLES

The gerontological social worker in a health care environment must have specialized knowledge of the aging process. This includes knowledge of the biology, psychology, and social functioning of people as they age. In addition, a social worker in health care must have a thorough knowledge of medical terminology, diseases of the elderly, mental illnesses, medications, treatment procedures, new medical technology, nutrition, audiology, physical therapy, occupational therapy, and speech therapy. The gerontological social worker's role in the health care setting requires specialized medical knowledge because it is essential to have information about diagnoses, diseases, prognoses, treatment procedures, and medications to understand their impact on an older person's functioning. Knowledge of drug interaction is crucial in understanding behavioral changes in a client. The gerontological social worker must have information about advances in medical technology when counseling a client who is undergoing a hip replacement or cataract surgery.

The medical social worker must be knowledgeable about how different states implement advance directives and health care proxies. The social worker must know local community resources. What resources are available in this particular community? Each community differs in the eligibility criteria for public programs. Is the patient eligible for Meals-on-Wheels? Are home repair services available to remodel the home of a person who uses a wheelchair? What are the criteria for eligibility for Medicaid and Medicare? Some states have long waiting lists for evaluation and restrict access to Medicaid-eligible services (e.g., nursing homes and adult day care services). Is there access to the services that the patient needs?

The social worker should have training in interdisciplinary collaboration and should be prepared to work with professionals from medicine, psychiatry, physiatry, dentistry, pharmacy, audiology, occupational therapy, nursing, nutrition, and health care administration. Coordination with professionals from various disciplines is necessary to help the patient's recovery. For example, knowledge of current research on treatments and diseases that affect older adults is essential for an accurate assessment of the patient's situation. Also, the social worker assesses family dynamics, such as the stress of caregiving for adult children and spouses, and social workers must be able to coordinate and access services from a very fragmented health care system.

The following list will give an idea of the many roles the medical social worker must fill:

- Social activism
- Social planning
- Administration
- Community organization
- Fund-raising
- Marketing
- Public relations
- Grant writing
- Counseling
- Planning
- Mediation
- Enabling
- Brokering
- Organizing

CASE EXAMPLE 1: A NEWLY ADMITTED NURSING HOME PATIENT

The following case example illustrates the application of generic principles of social work practice in a nursing home. The case demonstrates the variety of tasks a social worker performs in a nursing home. (Here and elsewhere, names have been changed.)

H. P. Wilcox is a 100-year-old man newly admitted to Magnolia Nursing Home in Charleston, South Carolina. He lived alone in a small house since his wife died 20 years ago. He was brought to Magnolia Nursing Home by his daughter, Rebecca Terra who is 75 years old and in poor health. Rebecca is a widow and lives in a three-room apartment downtown. She has a small Social Security pension to support herself. H. P.'s son John is 70 years old and lives in California. He is very concerned but is able to provide little assistance with H.P.'s care.

Mr. Wilcox has no acute medical problems and is mentally (cognitively) intact. He has a chronic urological problem and is incontinent of urine at times. He has some gastrointestinal problems which flare up occasionally, but he manages to control his discomfort with over-the-counter medications. His daughter, Rebecca, cooked his meals each day and a cleaning service was used to clean his house. In preparing for his future needs H.P. and Rebecca decided that the time had come for him to live in a safer environment and that she could no longer continue to help him with his care. At home he spent most of his day reading the newspaper, watching television, and playing solitaire.

H.P. came to the nursing home with a good attitude and retained his usual routines for a while. Three days after placement he fell in the bathroom. He did not have any serious injuries but had some bruises. The nursing staff cautioned him not to use the bathroom without calling for assistance. The following day, while in the shower, he became very aggressive and struck out at the aide assisting him. A psychiatrist prescribed a psychotropic medicine to calm him during "this period of adjustment."

The following week, he was not eating his meals and was sleeping most of the day. When awake, he was incoherent and lethargic. Rebecca was distraught about his mental and physical deterioration. In the fourth week of his placement, the social worker met with her to discuss his recent problems.

On the day of admission the social worker had written a complete social history. The social worker now interviewed H.P. again and prepared a comprehensive assessment of his current psychosocial functioning. The social worker's assessment was that H.P. Wilcox, a man who lived independently until age 100, was lethargic and uncommunicative after just 4 weeks of placement in this nursing home.

TEAM MEETING, CASE EXAMPLE 1

The following is the contribution of the team meeting.

Social worker: I am presenting the case of an elderly man who had been living in the community independently till age 100. I have prepared a copy of his social history for all of you. The presenting problem is: In 4 weeks of nursing home placement, Mr. Wilcox was first aggressive and now, after medication, is lethargic. His appetite is poor, and his family member (his daughter) is distraught over his deteriorating physical and mental condition.

Psychiatrist: Psychotropic medications which reduce a patient's aggressive behavior may have side effects such as lethargy. If we eliminate the medication, the staff must develop a plan to manage his behavior. This requires the cooperation of the social worker, nurse aide, recreation therapist, and family member.

Nurse: The patient is particularly aggressive during bathing and using the toilet. He struck a nurse aide while being washed and refuses help in the bathroom. He does not call for assistance to use the toilet and fell several times during the night shift.

Social worker: Can a male aide be assigned to help him with his bath? Can he use the toilet without supervision? He has managed to use a bathroom until age 100. He does not show any evidence of sight impairment, unsteady gait, or any medical condition which would put him at risk of falling. Is the light in his room adequate, so that he can see well? What kind of lighting did he have at home?

The team examined several approaches to help him and agreed that his use of the toilet and his bath should be handled by a male orderly. He had told his daughter that he was uncomfortable with young female nurse aides helping him with his bath and the toilet. He was monitored closely by the evening staff for the next few evenings. Within a few days, H.P.'s aggressive behavior decreased. He was permitted to take control of his environment. His appetite improved.

COMMENTS ON CASE 1

Case 1 illustrates the integration of principles of social work practice with specialized knowledge of older adults and settings—the framework for gerontological social work practice presented in this book. The importance of a comprehensive assessment which includes past behavior is illustrated. The function of the agency is to provide continuing care for H.P. Wilcox in a safe environment, and this function gives focus and direction to the work of the team. The team's discussion centers on how the agency's goal will be accomplished. The need for collaboration of team members from various disciplines (social work, nursing, and psychiatry) is evident. The social worker's relationship with the daughter is demonstrated as an essential aspect of the work, because in establishing a trusting relationship in which she can share her concerns about her father's care, the daughter becomes involved in the helping process. The social worker, after making an assessment of the problem, offers suggestions for changing the treatment of the patient. A social work perspective includes all of the patient's social factors and history to determine what may be the cause of the problem and how to resolve it. In this case the social worker determines that this 100-year-old man, widowed for 20 years, living alone, may not be comfortable with a young female bathing him and telling him what to do. The loss of control that is experienced in an institution must be recognized as a serious conflict for an older person, which can result in depression or sometimes in aggressive behavior. Potential conflict between the agency's needs and the client's needs was successfully resolved by the social worker. The nursing home social worker must be vigilant to the agency's function (to provide care) while recognizing the conflict between institutionalized care and individualized care in a system that is highly regulated by federal and state laws. The social worker helps the staff to explore alternative methods for meeting the individualized needs of the patient while protecting the institution, which must meet state and federal regulations for patients' safety and care.

QUESTIONS FOR DISCUSSION: CASE 1

1. What do you think is the social worker's primary task in this case?
2. Why do you think the social worker must develop a relationship with the daughter?
3. What information is necessary for the assessment?
4. What is the conflict between the client's needs and the agency's needs?
5. What is the social worker's most important task?
6. What would you do differently?
7. How does the agency's policy on the use of chemical restraints help or hinder a solution in this case?
8. How does the social worker use collaborative skills?
9. What specialized knowledge does the social worker need in this case?
10. What generic principles of social work are evident in this case?

CASE EXAMPLE 2: A CLIENT NEEDING ADDITIONAL SERVICES FROM COMMUNITY AGENCIES

The following case example is taken from the records of a home health care agency to illustrate gerontological social work practice in a home health care agency.

> Angela Allano is 89 years old. She was in Mercy Hospital for 3 weeks. Her diagnoses are congestive heart failure, hypertension, and aortic stenosis. She was discharged to her home in a medically stable condition. The hospital social worker referred her to a home health care agency for follow-up.

> Angela Allano lives alone in a one-family private house in a rural area. The patient's son Chris, age 65, and his family live 125 miles away, in the city. The son was present during the worker's visit to the home. He was very upset and concerned about his mother's inability to take care of herself. She refuses to live in his home in the city. She does not want to be a burden to her son and his family and insists on living in her own home. Mrs. Allano walks around the house with difficulty because she is short of breath. She is an anxious woman, and her son describes her as always having been nervous and tense. She is unable to shop for groceries or do any housekeeping chores. Mrs. Allano cannot attend doctor's appointments unescorted. Her deceased husband retired 40 years ago from the city police force, and she receives a police pension check ($500). She also has a monthly Social Security pension check of $350. Her monthly payments for her housing total $700. Thus she has a surplus of $150 monthly for additional expenses.

INTERVIEW, CASE EXAMPLE 2

Social worker:	Hello, Mrs. Allano, I am from the home health agency. I am here to see if you need any additional help in your home while you are recovering from your recent illness.
Angela Allano:	I can manage quite well. I can cook and take care of myself.
Social worker:	How will you manage to shop or do your laundry?
Angela Allano:	I may need a little help.
Social worker:	Can you bathe by yourself?
Angela Allano:	No.
Social worker:	Can I arrange for a homemaker to come to your home a few hours a day to do your shopping, cleaning, and laundry?
Angela Allano:	I would appreciate some help.
Social worker:	Do you have transportation to your doctor's office for follow-up appointments?

Angela Allano: No.

Social worker: How are you feeling since you left the hospital?

Angela Allano: I am short of breath when I exert myself. I am worried that if I don't get better, how I will manage to take care of myself? I am also a little sad that I need so much help. I have always been a very independent woman. I never thought this would happen to me. I hoped I would die before I became a burden to my son. I am sorry to be such a worry to my son.

Son: I have been here for 2 weeks now. I must get back to my job and family, but I am really concerned that Mom is here alone. I wish you would talk to her about living with me in the city. It is very difficult to help her from 125 miles away. My family would like her to live with us, but she refuses. I think she is being very stubborn and not realistic about what she can do after her last illness.

Social worker: Mrs. A, tell me how you feel about going to your son's house for a while until you are able to manage alone.

Angela Allano: No, this is my home. Although my son and his family are wonderful, I enjoy the privacy of my own home. I need to get up several times during the night to use the bathroom. I enjoy getting up early—5 a.m.—and having coffee. I nap during the day sometimes. I enjoy talking on the telephone to friends in different parts of the country. These are activities that are best done in your own home.

Social worker: Tell me what I can do to help you live safely and comfortably.

Angela Allano: I need some help at this time with housekeeping, meals, bathing, shopping, and trips to the doctor.

Social worker: I will arrange for some help with the chores we discussed, and that will ease your son's mind. I wonder if you have some friends we can call on to help also.

COMMENTS ON CASE 2

In case 2, a comprehensive assessment of the client and the home situation helped the social worker to determine the client's psychosocial needs and current level of functioning. The worker listens to the client's feelings about dependency and fears for the future, is empathic, and provides feedback. After determining that the client is cognitively intact, has some social supports, and can manage at home with some additional services, the social worker links the client with community agencies that can help with food preparation, such as the local Council on Aging. An assessment of the family indicates a strong relationship with the son which necessitates including the son in the helping process. The social worker also assesses the social support system of the client and involves the friends of the client in the helping process. A comprehensive assessment of the client's family, friends, and neighbors is essential in establishing a network of resources that can help the client's recovery and maintain the client at home. Coordination of social work services with other disciplines is necessary to provide the client with essential services for recovery. The social worker assesses the client's financial status to determine ability to pay for community programs such as Meals-on-Wheels and housekeeping. Most important in this case is the social worker's respect for the client's need for self-determination. The client decides what her needs are, and the social worker responds to meet those needs.

QUESTIONS FOR DISCUSSION: CASE 2

1. What specialized knowledge does the social worker need in this case?
2. What is the nature of the work to be accomplished?
3. Who are the other health care professionals who should be involved in this case?
4. What community resources are needed for this client?
5. What is the function of the agency?
6. Why is development of a relationship with the client necessary for the implementation of the work, and how is this accomplished?

CASE EXAMPLE 3: A FRAIL OLDER WOMAN IN A HOSPITAL

The following case illustrates social work practice in a hospital setting with an older woman.

> Catherine Michaels is 75 years old. She has been a patient at Saint Francis Hospital for 6 weeks. She has arthritis, osteoporosis, diabetes, arteriosclerotic heart disease, and hypertension. She has recovered from a kidney infection but is very debilitated. She is unable to walk, owing to severe osteoporosis, and uses a wheelchair. She is cognitively intact. She lives in a senior apartment housing development. Her physician recommends placement in a nursing home because of her multiple chronic conditions. Her three daughters agree that she should be placed in a nursing home. Catherine does not want to go to a nursing home. She wants to return to her own home, on a farm where she has lived for 50 years. The family does not

want her to be told that she is going to a nursing home. They want the staff, including the social worker, to tell her that she is going to a rehabilitation facility for a short period. They are very concerned that she will be depressed. The daughters and the doctor feel that they are making this decision in her best interest.

INTERVIEW, CASE EXAMPLE 3

The following is an excerpt from the social worker's interview with Catherine Michaels.

Social worker: Mrs. Michaels, I am the social worker assigned to the geriatric unit of the hospital. I understand you are to be discharged in a few days.

Catherine: Yes, I am feeling somewhat better but very weak. I can't walk without help.

Social worker: What plans have you made for your rehabilitation?

Catherine: Well, my doctor and my daughters have arranged for me to go to a rehab facility for a few weeks, until my strength returns.

Social worker: How do you feel about this plan?

Catherine: Well, I don't mind for a little while, but I definitely do not want to go to a nursing home. I want to return to my own home as soon as possible.

Social worker: Do you think you can take care of yourself in your own home? Do your daughters Anna and Teresa live nearby?

Catherine: They live close enough that I can call them if I need help in an emergency. However, I am very capable of calling for an ambulance if I am not feeling well.

Social worker: It seems that you have been ill very frequently recently, and your health care needs might require the help of skilled persons on a daily basis. Your daughters are worried that you are not getting adequate nursing care. Teresa has been calling me every day. They both seem very devoted to you. How do you feel about someone coming to your home to help?

Catherine: I would appreciate some help. I am happy at home. My friends from church visit and bring me special meals. My dog, Santo, is great company, and I have the freedom to make tea when I wish, watch television when I wish, and sit on my porch when the weather allows. I am happy with my life as it is now. I am prepared for it to end at some time and until it does, I am enjoying it.

COMMENTS ON CASE EXAMPLE 3

Case 3 illustrates the necessity of conducting a comprehensive assessment in working with older adults. Can she manage at home alone? Can she cook or shop? Who will help her? The client's social supports must not be overlooked. The agency's function gives direction to the work in that the social worker's task is to prepare a discharge plan for the client. However, the social worker cannot be effective if the worker is not aware of the client's wishes. A positive relationship is essential in developing a plan that the client and family will accept. Conflict between the client's wishes, the family's wishes, and the agency often can be resolved by the development of a relationship of trust with the family and the client. All of the team members must be involved in the care plan, and the expertise of each team member must be coordinated to develop a plan that is in the client's best interest (a primary standard of social work practice).

QUESTIONS FOR DISCUSSION: CASE EXAMPLE 3

1. To whom is the social worker responsible—client, agency, or family?
2. What must be included in the psychosocial assessment?
3. What are the ethical issues in this case?
4. How would you resolve this case? Should the client be placed in a nursing home or discharged home?
5. Who should decide where the client lives?
6. How is paternalism evident in this case?
7. What principles of social work are being violated in this case?
8. What is the function of the agency (the hospital)?
9. Which professionals would you include in a collaborative network to help this client?
10. What is the nature of the work with the client?

Gerontological social work practice in a health care environment requires specialized knowledge, but the principles of social work practice are the same in all settings of social work practice. Medicine is based on diagnosis. Social work is based on relationship. The development of a relationship with the client is what makes it social work. The social worker's primary responsibility is to the client. The ethics of the profession demand that the social worker respect the client's right to self-determination. The right must be carefully balanced against the client's need for protection. The social worker functions as an advocate, enabler, mediator, and planner. In health care settings the gerontological social worker requires specialized knowledge of medical treatment, diseases, diagnoses, medications, etc. The contract between worker and client must be determined by a principal value of the profession—the client's right to choose. Gerontological social work practice in a health care setting involves applying the principles outlined in this book. The integrative model that we have proposed for gerontological social work practice combines generalist principles with specialized knowledge of particular fields of practice such as the health care setting.

REFERENCES

Ferraro, K. (Ed.). (1990). *Gerontology: Perspectives and issues.* New York: Springer.

Hancock, B. (1990). *Social work with older people.* (2nd ed.). Englewood Cliffs, NJ: Prentice Hall.

Hooyman, N., & Kiyak, H.A. (1996). *Social gerontology.* (4th ed.). Boston: Allyn and Bacon.

Kim, P. (Ed.). (1990). *Serving the elderly.* New York: Aldine De Gruyter.

Moody, H.(1994). *Aging: Concepts and controversies.* Thousand Oaks, CA: Pine Forge.

CHAPTER 7

Social Work With the Aging in a Legal Environment

INTRODUCTION

The relationship between law and social work is very close, as evidenced by the fact that many law offices incorporate a social work staff position. In addition, many gerontological social workers in private practice develop collegial relations with "elder-lawyers" (lawyers who specialize in issues confronting older people) in order to provide more comprehensive service to clients. Social workers practicing in any area of health or delivery of social services must be attuned to the legal implications of clients' presenting problems. However, within the present theoretical framework, the distinction that characterizes the practice of social work in a legal environment is the focus of the task as defined by the organizational function or private practice contract. Gerontological social work in a legal environment is social work focusing on the provision of a social service that is ancillary to the delivery of a legal service. The need for the social work intervention derives from a legal matter. These legal matters include those related to estate planning and planning for retirement and long term care. In addition to services related to planning one's financial future, legal services tend to group themselves around health-related matters, such as living wills and health proxies.

This chapter addresses the role of the social worker in a legal environment. It includes a case example that describes an individual who is applying for Medicaid for home care.

WHAT IS GERONTOLOGICAL SOCIAL WORK
IN A LEGAL ENVIRONMENT?

Within the present frame of reference, gerontological social work in a legal environment is social work practiced with older adults in a legal setting. In its pure form, this would be the practice of social work in a private law office or a public legal aid office. It could also be social work in the criminal justice system—for example, a house of correction or a probation office. Practically speaking, however, much of private gerontological social work practice originates from some concerns about finances or retirement or some decision about health care that is essentially legal in nature. A client may be confused about what course to take in planning for incapacity or retirement, may have little or no awareness of his or her rights or entitlements, and may seek the assistance of a social worker to work out a plan. In reality, many of the presenting problems that motivate older adults to seek the assistance of a social worker are concrete, with financial and legal implications.

Acknowledging the close tie between the legal and social service aspects of their work, many gerontological social workers in private practice with older people have constructed their practices around the delivery of concrete services and refer to themselves as gerontological case managers. Many social workers in private practice regard themselves as psychiatric social workers but may emphasize the close coordination of mental health and legal professional tasks in the definition of professional function.

The gerontological social worker in a legal environment, to put it simply, is one who defines the work in terms of the delivery of specific psychosocial services that derive from legal or financial concerns.

PRINCIPLES

I.   Diagnosis or assessment of the client must be comprehensive and must include mental status, physical health, spiritual health, legal, and financial, and social condition.
II. The agency's function (or the contract with the client) gives direction and focus to the work.
III. Diagnosis or understanding of the client's need is most effective when related to the use of a particular service in the context of the client's relationship with the worker. In the case of the social worker in a legal environment (e.g., a criminal justice agency or law of-

fice), the particular service relates to the overall legal or correctional function or mission of the organization).

IV. Conscious use of administrative skills (e.g., time, policy, and strategic planning) promotes more effective delivery of service.

V. The relationship between the client and the worker, as defined by the function or contract, flows from the client's relationship with the agency or the "total client system" and can be used to promote both the interest of the particular client and the interest of the client's representative social group.

VI. Conscious use of collaborative skills promotes more effective delivery of services.

THE WORKER'S ROLE

The worker's role in the legal setting or within the context of a legal problem or concern is distinguished from work in other contexts solely by the nature of the presenting issue. The social worker performs the same tasks regardless of setting. The worker begins by making a comprehensive assessment of the client's biopsychosocial condition. The worker contracts with the client or client group to provide help with a particular problem that has a legal foundation. The work consists of an application of the generic principles outlined above. The worker will attend to both individual and systems issues in the performance of his or her role and will employ a range of skills in diagnosis, communication and administration. The issues that present themselves in the legal environment may range from financial and social concerns surrounding the need to plan for incapacity to issues related to estate planning and planning for retirement.

CASE EXAMPLE: AN OLDER APPLICANT FOR MEDICAID FOR HOME CARE

The following case example is presented to highlight the role of the social worker as mediator in conflicts between an older person and his or her family. The case reflects the importance of collaboration with an "elder lawyer" and the use of collaborative techniques. The case also demonstrates the importance of biopsychosocial assessment in the development of a helping strategy.

Tom Cilli is an 82-year-old Italian American man who lived with his wife in a private house in Queens, New York, until her death 1 year ago. His income consists of his pension and Social Security totaling $1815 per month; and interest from approximately $200,000 in savings. His only other major asset is the house, which is valued at approximately $175,000. Mr. Cilli is suffering from congestive heart failure and diabetes. He is not strong enough to perform certain activities of daily living, including cleaning, shopping, and cooking. His physical condition is degenerating, and it is apparent that within the next several months he will require additional supportive services, including help with personal hygiene and physical mobility.

Mr. Cilli has been paying out of pocket for a home attendant to come in twice a week to assist with shopping, cleaning and cooking. The cost—$100 per week has been drawn from his savings account. Mr. Cilli's daughter, Connie Petrone, sought the services of an elder lawyer, Jean Farber, to discuss her father's eligibility for Medicaid for home care. The attorney referred Connie to a social worker who serves as a social service consultant for the law office. The purpose of the referral was to evaluate the options for Mr. Cilli's continued care and to identify areas of agreement and disagreement among principal family members in deciding on a long term plan.

CASE EXAMPLE: FIRST INTERVIEW

The following process recording represents the worker's first interview with Connie Petrone.

Worker: Can you fill me in on what you and Ms. Farber have been discussing regarding your father's situation? Do you understand what her reasons were for sending you to speak with me?

Connie: My father is deteriorating and we—my husband and I—don't know how he's going to manage financially and personally when he gets really bad. I thought we'd apply for Medicaid, but I understand it's not so easy. I think Ms. Farber thought you could help me figure something out?

Worker: What were her thoughts about Medicaid and home care?

Connie: Well, he couldn't qualify now, with what he has in the bank. He'd have to transfer it over to either me or my brother. My brother is—I don't know how to put this. ...He's a gambler, he's not married; we don't hear from him unless he needs something.... but my father is too easy with him. When my mother was alive, she kept control of the purse strings; but now my father is capable of giving everything he's got to Frankie, who would spend it on himself. It's not that my father isn't

	thinking straight.... It's just that he feels responsible or something. I don't know why I'm going off on this tangent.... I probably didn't answer your question.
Worker:	I guess you're telling me how complicated the situation is.
Connie:	Yes, I guess so. Ms. Farber said there are ways of protecting the house.... It's all paid off, and maybe we could protect the savings.... But then there's the issue of whether Dad should go to a nursing home or we should try to arrange additional home care. My husband doesn't want him living with us because of his relationship with Frankie. I guess I don't know what I'm talking about.
Worker:	Why do you say that? You're being very clear; it's just that the situation is complicated.
Connie:	I guess I'm confused?
Worker:	Are you confused? Do you have any thoughts about what you'd like to see happen here?
Connie:	I'd like to sell the house, move my father in with me, and get some home care.... But my husband doesn't want that...you know, because of Frankie.
Worker:	Is it just Frankie, or does anything else bother him about that plan?
Connie:	He doesn't admit it, but look... he wants his privacy. John works hard; he sells insurance. He likes to come home to some peace. Our older daughter just moved back in with us—she lost her job and the younger boys are in college. John Jr. is in graduate school. Even with the loans it still costs us plenty for room and board and part of the tuition.
Worker:	Do you have a job?
Connie:	I work in the local library part-time. I have a lot to do at home still, particularly with my daughter there now. My sons come home every weekend. You know how it is—sometimes they bring their girlfriends.
Worker:	Maybe you could use a little privacy too?
Connie:	Believe me, it's not that I want my father to move in with us.... He's eighty-two. I feel obligated.
Worker:	Has anyone discussed any of this with your father?
Connie:	Only the Medicaid.... He says he's not applying for welfare.
Worker:	Perhaps I should speak with your father. There are several options for his care, besides home care or a nursing home. He may be more suited for an adult home, for instance. But someone ought to let him know. Does he know about his failing physical condition?
Connie:	I think he knows.... We don't say too much; we don't want to frighten him.
Worker:	How would you feel about my talking with him?
Connie:	I wish you would.
Worker:	You say that, but he's going to have thoughts of his own and he's got a right to make certain decisions for himself.

Connie:	Look, as long as he doesn't turn everything over to my brother, it's his life; he can do what he wants.
Worker:	Does your father have a will?
Connie:	Yes.
Worker:	Did he leave everything to your brother?
Connie:	No. As far as I know everything is equally divided between me and my brother.
Worker:	So why do you think he can be so easily influenced by your brother now?
Connie:	My brother knows how to manipulate him.
Worker:	What does he do?
Connie:	I think he plays on his guilt. My brother didn't finish college. He says it's because my father didn't give him the money. That's not true. He was playing the horses instead of going to class.
Worker:	Does he have any kind of employment?
Connie:	He's a shoe salesman.... He makes a living, I guess.
Worker:	Connie, if we work out some plan that meets with your father's approval and he gets settled, will that take care of things for you right now?
Connie:	That's all I'm asking for, are you a psychotherapist?
Worker:	I am a certified social worker. Why do you ask?
Connie:	I'd just like to know.... You asked me if this would settle things for me. Right now that's all I'm asking.... Maybe later you can help me with something else; we'll see.
Worker:	We'll begin with my arranging to visit your dad. Then we'll take it from there.

COMMENTS ON THE CASE EXAMPLE: FIRST INTERVIEW

The first interview illustrates the worker's effort to develop a contract with the client (who in this case is the daughter of the older person) and to mediate between the needs of the client, Connie, and the needs of her father, Tom. In this instance, there doesn't appear to be any conflict of interest between Connie and Tom. However, Frank appears to represent a threat to harmonious relations. The worker's focus with Connie is to help her acknowledge her own agenda for her father so that the father will have a clear understanding of the options for his continued care. If a transfer of money is involved in the planning, then the lawyer will handle the legal details. Federal legislation, effective January 1997, governing transfers of assets for Medicaid eligibility imposes criminal penalties on individuals who transfer funds for the purpose of becoming eligible for medical assistance—if disposing of the funds results in an imposition of a period of ineligibility for Medicaid (Title 42, Public Health and Welfare; Chapter 7, Social Security;

Subchapter XI, General Provisions and Peer Review). In addition, depending on the provisions of the state's Medicaid law, a house may be an exempt asset in Medicaid considerations of eligibility in certain specific instances. Examples of such instances are situations in which the older person is expected to return home after a nursing home admission, or a spouse or dependent child occupies the house while the owner is in a nursing home. Furthermore, decisions to establish Medicaid eligibility by means of a transfer or trust arrangement must weigh the cost of extended care against the tax cost incurred in the transaction. This underscores the importance of legal consultation in matters related to entitlement eligibility.

The collaborative relationship between the lawyer and the social worker in this case example demonstrates their mutual understanding of each other's role in planning. The lawyer will have oversight responsibility for any matters related to the sale of the house or application for benefits, such as Medicaid, as well as for all matters pertaining to eligibility for admission to a nursing home or an adult home. The lawyer and the social worker have a clear concept of their respective tasks. This eases relations between them and promotes more effective service delivery. The social worker will help to identify the best plan and will coordinate home care services, if necessary, or help in the selection of a nursing home. The social worker will be available in all phases of the process to identify areas of disagreement among family members and help facilitate a plan that primarily represents Tom's best interest without ignoring the client's (Connie's) interest. This case raises many questions for the social worker which require both ethical and technical solutions.

QUESTIONS FOR DISCUSSION: CASE EXAMPLE, FIRST INTERVIEW

1. If Connie is the client, what should the worker do if the interests of Tom and Connie are irreconcilable?
2. How would Smalley's principle that diagnosis is most effective when related to the use of the service apply in this situation? Who is the subject of assessment in this case: Connie, Tom, the family, or each individual in the family?
3. Do you agree that Connie is the client?
4. What would happen to the house if Tom suddenly had to go to a nursing home for the remainder of his life?
5. Who should have the final say regarding Tom's ultimate disposition, his son Frank or his daughter Connie?

THE PRINCIPLE OF CONSENT

The individual's right of consent is central to the laws applying to making decisions about health care (Harron, Burnside, & Beauchamp, 1983). This includes decisions having to do with planning for continuity of care. Examples include decisions regarding nursing home or adult home admission. *No one has the right to make decisions for a competent adult, including the spouse.* Although it is typically assumed that the marital partner has this right, this is not true. In addition, only a judge or a court-appointed guardian or committee has the legal right to make decisions about treatment or health planning for another person. A person is considered competent unless deemed incompetent in a court of law. This is true even if a person is diagnosed with a severe mental or cognitive impairment. However, there are certain exceptions to this rule, which relate to the appointment of a health proxy, the signing of a living will, or the signing of "do-not-resuscitate" orders. These advance directives are legal protections designed for individuals who have lost their mental capacity. They provide instructions for decisions about health care. There are variations among the states in the laws regarding health care decision making and this underscores the need for legal consultation.

Some legal protections are designed to provide another individual with the authority to make financial decisions only. The durable power of attorney represents such an option and is a useful mechanism for ensuring continuity in the management of a person's financial resources in the event of mental or physical incapacity. A durable power of attorney can avoid the necessity of a lengthy court proceeding.

ELIGIBILITY FOR ENTITLEMENTS

As already suggested, one area which is very complicated has to do with eligibility requirements for Medicaid for home care or nursing home services. The laws have many provisions, such as the community "spouse resource allowance," the right of a spouse to refuse community or institutional Medicaid, periods of ineligibility for Medicaid in cases involving transfers of assets, and types and hours of covered home care.

These laws have an impact on older people's need to plan financially for incapacity, and, again, they frequently make legal consultation necessary. The social worker in a legal setting is instrumental in helping older people come to terms with the necessity of planning for incapacity and in mediating in any family conflicts that may arise in the process.

ELDER ABUSE

Older people are at risk of all kinds of abuse because of their increased physical dependency. Financial abuse is one common type of abuse. Often the abuser is a child who is dependent on a parent for financial or emotional support. Their relationship is thus characterized by codependency. Self-interest may be at the core of a potential heir's agenda for an older person's continued care or estate plan.

The presenting issue in the case of Tom Cilli is financial, although it is patently clear that the situation is also fraught with other conflicts and risks. Tom will become increasingly vulnerable to family pressures as his health deteriorates. Since his daughter Connie is the client in this situation, the social worker must recognize any potential conflict of interest. The social worker could face an ethical dilemma as the case unfolds. This dilemma is illustrated in the interview with Tom Cilli that is presented below.

CASE EXAMPLE: SECOND INTERVIEW

The interview here is the worker's follow-up diagnostic evaluation of Tom Cilli. The purpose of the interview is to evaluate his understanding of his physical condition and review options for his continued care.

Worker:	Tom, I have come to your home at the request of your daughter, Connie, who is concerned about your ability to manage by yourself and would like me to talk with you about your concerns for yourself. Do you have any questions to ask me?
Tom:	You say my daughter is concerned about me. I don't know why. I manage to get things done for myself. I have a woman coming in to help a few days a week. I do all right.
Worker:	So you're saying you don't have any concerns about how you're managing?
Tom:	Well, sure I have concerns.... Wouldn't anyone? I just don't see the point in talking about it.
Worker:	Well, maybe there is nothing we can discuss that can help, but would you give me a chance to ask you a few questions? Sometimes I make a suggestion that is helpful.
Tom:	I don't mind talking to you.
Worker:	Tom, the reason your daughter is concerned is that she feels that even though you're managing for yourself now, down the road you may require more assistance than you're getting. How would you describe your physical health?
Tom:	I'm not so good.

Worker:	Are you finding it more difficult to do anything in particular?
Tom:	My energy seems to be going. I have trouble with my leg now; it causes me a lot of pain because of the swelling.
Worker:	So you must be worried.
Tom:	Who wouldn't be? Look, young lady, I can tell you it's not easy to get old.
Worker:	You think I may not know that?
Tom:	You're young; you don't have to deal with these things. That's good. But as for me, that's another story. So what can you suggest, the fountain of youth?
Worker:	I wish.... Well, even though it's not everything you might wish for, sometimes knowing what to expect and planning can give a person a little sense of security. Have you thought about what might happen if you couldn't continue to manage?
Tom:	I guess I'd have to get more help. I've discussed it with my son, Frank. He's single and has offered to come live with me. My daughter isn't going to like that. Did she mention Frank to you?
Worker:	She did. What are your thoughts about why she wouldn't like the plan?
Tom:	She thinks he's no good. He's had some trouble.
Worker:	What do you think?
Tom:	I think he's offering to stay with me!
Worker:	And?
Tom:	Nobody else is offering to put me up.
Worker:	You mean Connie isn't offering?
Tom:	She's got her own life, but my generation was different....you took care of your own.
Worker:	So you think your son's your only option? Do you think it would be a good idea to have him in your home?
Tom:	I don't know. He's not that bad. It's just that he's always hitting me up for money. I don't like that.
Worker:	What if we could arrange for additional home care? Do you think that would be better than having Frank move in?
Tom:	In some ways I'd rather deal with Frank.
Worker:	Can you explain what would make it better to have Frank around?
Tom:	That's just the point—I'd have him around. I get lonely,... and if I can't get out to the Senior Center, then what. I'll be stuck home with a stranger all day.
Worker:	Your wife died last year. I can imagine that you really miss her at these times when you feel alone.
Tom:	She was the lucky one; she went first.
Worker:	You feel so bad that you wish you had gone before her?
Tom:	Yes, I do.... But what makes it worse is my daughter's attitude. She'd probably like to put me in a nursing home to get rid of me.
Worker:	You're angry with her!

Tom:	I know she's not all bad.
Worker:	Tom, you don't have to go to a nursing home. There may be a way to get you some extra help at home and also see that you continue to get out to be with people. You know your Senior Center has a day care program for adults who can't get around on their own. They could even pick you up in a van and return you home at the end of the day. Even if your health deteriorates, as long as you can still get out, we could try to arrange some activities for you. Do you understand what I'm saying?
Tom:	Is this what Connie wants?
Worker:	Is it important to you what she wants?
Tom:	Well, that's what's going to be, isn't it?
Worker:	What do you want, Tom?
Tom:	I don't know. I don't know any more.
Worker:	I hear your helplessness.
Tom:	It's a pity what happens to people. (Momentary silence.) I know you're just trying to help. It just seems useless.
Worker:	Would anything I can do help a little?
Tom:	What do you suggest?
Worker:	I guess I did say I give suggestions. Do you think we could talk again? Maybe it would be a good idea to talk all this over with your children present.
Tom:	You think Connie will do that?
Worker:	Yes, I do. What about Frank?
Tom:	We'll see....I'd have to ask him. Maybe it's not such a good idea to have them come together.
Worker:	Well, then, we can talk with them separately. By the way, I understand you think that Medicaid is like welfare. Can we talk about that for a minute?
Tom:	Isn't Medicaid like welfare? Don't you have to be poor to get Medicaid?
Worker:	Well, you can't be rich. (Both laugh.)... Medicaid is a way that you might be able to afford some home care if you don't have the money. A lot of people qualify for it. Right now you might be able to protect some of your savings, but it involves transferring assets to one or both of your children.... We should talk about that some more too.
Tom:	You mean my children would have control over my money?
Worker:	Otherwise, it could all get spent on home care, if you need it. It's a legal way of protecting the money.
Tom:	I'm not sure I understand, but which child would get the money?
Worker:	That's something we have to discuss further. I know Connie doesn't think Frank is a good choice.
Tom:	I don't know if I want to discuss this with my children yet.

COMMENTS ON THE SECOND INTERVIEW

This second interview reveals the complexity of the issues surrounding any plan for Tom's continuing care. His son Frank has offered to live with him, but even Tom isn't clear about Frank's motives. Connie, who appears to be the more trustworthy candidate, is experiencing her own conflicts regarding her father's long term management. The social worker has to evaluate whether she can mediate between the different interests without sacrificing Tom's right to direct the course of his own life.

QUESTIONS FOR DISCUSSION: SECOND INTERVIEW

1. If Connie is the client, can the social worker do justice to Tom's concerns?
2. What factors would be important to consider in an assessment of Tom's biopsychosocial condition?
3. How does Connie's perception of the problem differ from her father's? Can the worker use her knowledge of this difference to the advantage of both individuals? Is there any way that Frank's agenda can be brought into agreement with that of his sister?
4. If the worker's relationship with the client can be used to benefit both the client and the client's representative group, what are the implications for the worker's role?
5. What would be your strategic plan in working on this case, for example, definition of problems, objectives, and methods of achieving objectives?

ADVOCACY VERSUS MEDIATION

The line between advocacy and mediation reflects a basic difference in perspective regarding human nature. Schwartz and Zalba (1971) wrote very eloquently about the concept of identifying common ground between the purposes of clients (or client groups) and the purposes of the agencies in which they are served. Other writers have outlined more partisan processes of confronting opposition to the client's interest through adversarial or political action (Brager & Holloway, 1978; Kahn, 1979). Lawyers tend to be adversarial. Social workers tend to look for the point of compromise among competing interests, believing that human beings are basically willing to compromise. This difference in perspective can create complications for a lawyer and social worker who are working together on a case.

In the Cilli case, Connie is the lawyer's client. If Connie wishes to fight her brother for the right to manage her father's financial activities, the lawyer would represent Connie. The social worker may take a different view and try to achieve family consensus or may actually feel obligated to counteract the lawyer's efforts if the older person's interests are in jeopardy. Social work is a profession that is dedicated to advancing the rights of the underprivileged or vulnerable in society. Here, not only must the social worker mediate between the interests of the various family members; she also must find some common ground between her plan for the client and the lawyer's plan. If the social worker cannot represent Connie's position without balancing it with Tom's position, than one option would be for her to refer Tom to another social worker who will put his interest first. These conflicts can be minimized through clear communication and cooperative strategic planning by professionals. However, the worker should be guided as much by ethical principles as by principles of good practice.

THE MEANING OF THE REPRESENTATIVE GROUP

One principal responsibility of the social worker is to promote not only the interest of the client but also the interest of the client's *representative group*. This means that all social workers are obligated to influence agency or institutional policy.

A social worker who is employed in a law office is a member of a host agency. This means that the organization is not likely to be organized on the basis of ideological principles of social work. However, a social worker in a law office can influence organizational policy to the advantage of his or her clients through a variety of means. The social worker may institute a routine screening system in which all older clients are assessed according to comprehensive health and social criteria. In addition, gerontological social workers in a legal environment may become active on professional task forces devoted to shaping Medicare or Medicaid policy, promoting antidiscriminatory employment policies, or protecting elders from abuse.

The fact that should be emerging with increasing clarity is that the only distinctions between the practice of gerontological social work in a legal environment and other forms of social work practice are the age of the population served and the focus of the work. These distinctions require the worker to have specialized knowledge of the biopsychosocial condition of older people, specialized knowledge of the laws and legislative policies that affect their need for legal services, and a general understanding of the role of social work in the legal environment and the associated tasks. These tasks range from individual diagnostics and helping to administration and strategic planning. They are the same regardless of setting. Smalley's framework provides a comprehensive framework for integrating these different tasks.

REFERENCES

Brager, G., & Holloway, S. (1978). *Changing human service organizations.* (1978) New York: Free Press.

Harron, F., Burnside, J., & Beauchamp, T. (1983). *Health and human values.* New Haven, CT: Yale University Press.

Kahn, A. (1973). *Shaping the new social work.* New York: Columbia University Press.

Schwartz, W., & Zalba, S. (1971). *The practice of group work.* New York: Columbia University Press.

CHAPTER 8

Gerontological Social Work Practice in a Religious Environment

INTRODUCTION

The social work profession is taking a renewed interest in social work practice and religion (Popple, 1996). Brashears and Roberts (1996), however, report that "social work practice in the church is rarely mentioned in the professional literature" (p. 181). Although social work practice has its history in religion, the secularization of social work has separated it from the church for over 40 years (Popple, 1996).

Social workers are traditionally persons who want to help others, and historically they were religious persons. Early social workers were ministers, priests, and nuns. For many centuries churches were involved in charitable works in hospitals, communities, and other institutions. The church's mission was to help the poor, the aged, the infirm, and the homeless. In 1935, with the passage of the Social Security Act, the government became the primary source of social support in the United States. In the 1960s and 1970s, government programs assumed responsibility for many of the tasks that had once been borne by religious organizations, such as helping the poor, the aged, the ill, and the homeless. Popple offers an interesting explanation of the trend toward secularization. He suggests that at one time moral deficiencies were viewed as the causes of social problems such as poverty and unemployment. However, social work believed that society—not the moral weakness of the individual—was to blame for social problems. This belief led to the separation of morality and spiritual issues from social work

87

practice. Social workers turned to science and research for explanations for society's problems. As the government assumed responsibility for social issues, the primary function of religion became spiritual issues.

However, in today's climate of political conservatism, religion has once again emerged as a source of social service support and Popple reports a reversal of the trend toward secularization. Because government programs cannot meet the needs of the poor, the ill, and the homeless, religion is once again being considered a source of support for its members. Religious organizations can be a vital source for the provision of social services for many Americans.

In 1994, 59 percent of Americans reported that religion is very important in their lives, and 64 percent stated that they believed religion can answer all or most of today's problems (Popple, 1996). The role of the church in African American culture is described by Logan (1996), who holds that Black Americans are the most religious group in the world. Logan notes that at the time she was writing, 81 percent of Black Americans were church members and 78 percent believed that religion was important in their lives.

Evidence that the social work profession is taking a renewed interest in social work in the religious environment can be found in journals such as *Social Work and Christianity,* and in numerous articles, such as Doka (1986); Filinson (1988); and Abbott, Garland, Huffman-Nevins, and Stewart (1990). Still, the question is being asked, "Should the religions be involved in social work and social welfare?" We believe that religion has a social responsibility to assist those in need, and older adults and their families are in need of social supports.

RELIGION AND OLDER ADULTS

Religious gerontology is the study of the spiritual and religious needs of older adults. The research literature indicates that *religiosity* (defined as membership in a religious organization) and *spirituality* (defined as individual practices or belief in a higher being) are very important to older adults (Tobin, Ellor, & Anderson-Ray, 1986). Spirituality is further defined by the National Interfaith Coalition on Aging as the "affirmation of life in a relationship with God, self, community, and environment that nourishes and celebrates wholeness."

Studies indicate that being religious is positively related to well-being and morale in older persons (Hooyman & Kiyak, 1993). The evidence suggests that four out of five persons over 65 attend church or synagogue regularly (Tobin et al., 1986). There are no differences in gender: both men and women report that spirituality is related to their well-being and life satisfaction. It is implied in the literature that religious beliefs and spirituality tend to increase after age 60 (Hooyman and Kiyak, 1993). Moberg (1975) found that older persons are affiliated with religious organizations more often than with all other types of voluntary social organizations combined. Cultural studies suggest that African American older adults are more involved in religion than their White counterparts, and there is evidence that church membership is an integral part of the life of many older African Americans (Taylor, 1993). For many African Americans churches provide a variety of social services such as transportation, meals, clothing, support groups, and financial assistance.

SOCIAL WORK PRACTICE
IN THE RELIGIOUS ENVIRONMENT

This chapter examines gerontological social work practice in the religious environment. Here, *religious environment* refers specifically to churches and synagogues.

We believe that religious organizations can be vital sources of support for older adults and their families from a social work perspective as well as a spiritual perspective. In today's society, with its limited resources, the government is not completely able to provide for a growing aging population. (The population over age 65—31 million people—now represents 13% of the total population of the United States, and it is expected to growing at an unprecedented rate (Statistical Abstracts, 1993). Religion can be a valuable resource in the provision of social services to an aging population. Within the last decade, some religious organizations have begun to recognize their value as social supports for older adults and some denominations have developed social welfare programs for older persons. However, much more could be done, and gerontological social workers can be a vital link in this helping process.

In a religious setting, social work practice involves having specialized knowledge about religious denominations and the organization of religious institutions as well an ability to work with members of the clergy (e.g., ministers, priests, and rabbis), with religious boards, with laypeople, and with others in the hierarchy of a religious organization.

Religious organizations such as churches are, of course, in cities and in rural areas. The social worker in a religious setting must have specialized knowledge about the culture, the finances, and the physical and social environment of the congregation. A religious organization may recognize its responsibility to its older members, but its leaders often need assistance and training in assessing community needs; planning educational programs for older adults (such as Medicare and long-term-care insurance); linking services to community agencies (for example, mental health community services, food stamp programs, and home care agencies); implementing new programs (such as day care and respite programs); and issues of aging. Social workers can collaborate with religious leaders to provide essential social services to older persons.

Brashears and Roberts (1996) report on an innovative social service program of the Second Baptist Church in Kansas City, Missouri. The Second Baptist Church is the oldest African American Baptist church in Kansas City and has 700 members. In 1987 a social worker was added to the church staff in a part-time paid position. The social worker is described as developing "a generalist practice of providing direct services to the members of the church and their families, as well as serving as program administrator in the church's organizational structure" (p. 185). The social worker's duties were direct services such as:

Case management for elderly and disabled members

Support services to homebound and institutionalized members

Support services to members and families experiencing distress, health crises, and death

Family support services

Community requests for emergency assistance

Administrative functions included these:

Development and implementation of educational workshops and materials for members in the community

Coordination of social service activities with other organizations and programs within the church

Acting as a field instructor for social service practicuum students and as a consultant with seminary students in placement at the church for field training

Both micro- and macro-level activities are the domain of social work practice in the religious environment.

THE WORKER'S ROLES

Social workers have many roles in the religious environment. They are brokers, advocates, mediators, counselors, educators, planners, and consultants. They work with individuals, families, groups, other organizations, and community leaders. A social worker can link older persons with community agencies. For example, older people may confide in a priest, minister or rabbi about abuse by an adult child, although fear or shame may prevent them from reporting abuse to the police. A social worker makes assessments, plans interventions, and links the family to an appropriate community agency for ongoing counseling. Here is another example: A minister may note a change in attitude in a long time church member. The person is not coming to services as regularly, seems to be more isolated, is less communicative and is at times poorly groomed. A social worker makes a comprehensive assessment and determines mild depression and refers the person to a local community mental health clinic for treatment.

Social workers provide casework services and run group programs in religious settings. For example, most communities have families who are caring for people with Alzheimer's disease, but few communities have support groups. Support groups for caregivers are effective in delaying institutionalization (Penrod, Kane, & Finch, 1995). Social workers can lead or teach others to lead such support groups. Members of religious congregations (social workers, psychologists, therapists) can lead support groups sponsored by those organizations. Support groups for widows and widowers, caregivers, and people who are living with cancer or other diseases help families deal with the stresses of caregiving. Group programs for persons with chronic or life-threatening diseases are usually offered in medical settings, but religious groups can offer such programs in a religious environment.

Issues of death and dying can be a focus of religious organizations as well as medical or legal institutions. However, decisions about life support are no longer the domain of religious leaders. Physicians and lawyers monitor these decisions. Social workers can take the lead by offering individual counseling on advance directives and bereavement, and by developing support groups for people who have lost a loved one or who need to adjust to some life crisis, such as the onset of Alzheimer's disease in a spouse.

Social work practice in religious settings can involve individuals, groups, or the community. Social planning, community organizing and social advocacy are skills of social work practice that can be effectively used in collaboration with religious leaders. In this time of shrinking government resources, collaboration between religious leaders, religious organizations, congregants, and community providers is essential. For example, transportation is a vital issue for older persons, and in both rural and urban communities lack of transportation for older persons is often a major barrier to access to services. How can an older person come to a church or synagogue, for instance—or to medical and dental appointments—if transportation is not available? Some more progressive congregations own vans and provide daily transportation services. What other programs can religious groups develop to solve the transportation problems of older adults? Some public agencies use mobile vans that bring older people to houses of worship around the state for health screenings, resource assessment, information, and referral (Private communication, 1996).

Social workers can work with religious organizations to develop programs for social services (such as mental health counseling programs and home-delivered meals). There is evidence that community services are frequently underutilized by older persons because they are not "user-friendly" in some areas, especially for minority elders (Brashears & Roberts, 1996).

"Program development is a natural outcome of macro social work change" (Brueggemann, 1996, p. 278). Developing a program includes working with a board of directors, locating funding for the program, developing its structure and staffing. In addition, the process must involve social planning with community leaders.

Religious organizations have an opportunity and a responsibility to reach out to persons in need. They also have a cadre of experts in their membership (doctors, nurses, social workers, educators). Among the membership of a church or synagogue, for example, are physicians, nurses, social workers, teachers, therapists, etc., who can provide essential services to older persons under the auspices of the congregation. The experience of the Second Baptist Church in Kansas City demonstrates how social work practice can be successfully integrated in a religious environment. The gap in service delivery will widen as the population ages unless religious groups and community agencies link together in collaborative efforts to plan for older adults.

The tasks of the social worker in the Second Baptist Church in Kansas City illustrate social work practice in a religious environment. One of the social services provided by the social worker at the Second Baptist Church in Kansas City was case management for elderly and disabled members of the church. The goal of this service was to prevent institutionalization and to sustain independence. The service ministries of the church provided in-home services. Support services were given to homebound and institutionalized members. Clothing was provided when needed. The social worker contacted social service departments and administrators of institutions. Legal guardians were available for those who needed them. The social worker worked with hospital discharge planners to arrange for in-home services or nursing home placements. Meetings were arranged with the hospital staff and family members. Grief counseling was offered. Families received assistance with financial matters with insurance companies, doctors' offices, hospitals, government agencies, and funeral homes. Family help was offered to all members of the church. The social worker provided information and referral for career counseling, employment and educational opportunities, location of child care facilities, and family and individual counseling. The social worker assessed resources for those members who requested financial assistance from the church. Since the church had a social service function, other duties included overseeing the social service functions of the church (the annual budget, annual reports, and meetings of church committees). The social worker developed a 52-page guide of resources for seniors which was available to the members of the church.

The following cases describe application of the principles of social work practice in a religious setting as presented in this book. In this conceptual framework, generic principles of social work practice based on functionalism are integrated with specialized knowledge of aging and settings. This concept cuts across the practice areas and provides an orientation to casework, group work, and community organization.

CASE EXAMPLE 1: A CHURCH MEMBER HAVING TROUBLE WITH ALCOHOL

The first case illustrates how the social worker's skill in assessment and diagnosis is integrated with knowledge of aging.

> Joseph T. is 65 years old. He has been involved in the church intermittently throughout his life in the town where he has lived for 35 years. His wife died 2 years ago. She was an active church member. He lives in a small house alone, having retired from a management position in state government at age 62. His daughter, Teresa L., lives nearby with her family and visits him several times a week. She is also an active church member and is very involved in church activities. The minister is the Reverend Peter M.

INTERVIEWS: CASE 1

Teresa L. (daughter):   I came to see you, Pastor M., because I am concerned about my father.
Minister (Peter M.):   I hope I can help and offer you some guidance.
Teresa L.:   When I visit Dad, I find several bottles of beer and liquor throughout the house. Sometimes he seems so tired and hardly speaks to me, and at other times he is very outgoing and happy. I think he is drinking too much.
Peter M.:   Have you asked him if he is having a problem with drinking ?
Teresa L.:   No. I wonder if you can do that. It's really hard for me to talk to him and tell him I think he has a drinking problem. Dad was an alcoholic 20 years ago. Since my mother died, he seems to have slipped back into drinking. Can you help him?
Peter M.:   No, but I would like to call a social worker from a local family services agency to visit him and assess the situation. The social worker may decide that he needs a referral to the Barnwell Community Mental Health Center for treatment.

The minister informs the social worker of the situation.

Social worker: Yes, I think I can help, but first, I would like to visit with Joseph T. to make an assessment of his current functioning. I would also need to prepare a social history to determine influencing factors, coping behaviors, medical condition, family history, mental status, and social supports. I want to meet with his daughter to obtain her input on the problem and learn more about his past.

(The social worker now interviews Joseph T.)

Social worker: Mr. T., I have been asked to come here to discuss your daughter's and your minister's concerns. They seem to feel that since your wife died your behavior has changed and you may be having a problem with alcohol.
Joseph T.:   Well, since my wife died, I have been very lonely. Time passes very slowly each day. I am not sleeping well, and I have a drink at night to help me sleep. I really don't drink very much. One or two beers. It's something to dull the pain.
Social worker: Is this a habit you have had all your life, or a more recent one?
Joseph T.:   No, I started after my wife died. When she was alive, we were very busy, and I had no problem sleeping. I really don't know what to do with myself all day. I have no friends, and my children are very busy. They are wonderful children, but they have their own families.

Social worker: What do you do each day?

Joseph T.: Well, I read the newspaper in the morning, shop a little, cook a little, and watch television until I go to bed.

Social worker: When you have had problems in the past, how have you coped with them?

Joseph T.: My wife and I shared problems and worked together for solutions, but we didn't have many problems with our children or anything else.

Social worker: Were you and your wife active socially?

Joseph T.: My wife and I traveled, went out to restaurants, and shopped together. I really don't know how to function without her. I feel as if my life is over.

Social worker: I can understand how you feel this way. You've suffered a great loss.

Joseph T.: I am very lonely. I'm not coping well.

Social worker: Tell me how you're not coping.

Joseph T.: I'm falling apart, letting the house go,... having an occasional drink. I really shouldn't drink at all. I have been on the wagon 20 years. I just don't seem to care what happens.

COMMENTS ON CASE 1

Family members frequently seek help from the clergy, but although clergy-men and -women may have some training in counseling, they usually do not have specialized training in addictions. Alcoholism in older adults requires specialized knowledge, since there is a great deal of new information on alcohol abuse and older persons that suggests preferred treatment methods and links depression and losses to alcohol abuse in older persons. (Osgood, Wood, & Parham, 1995). Gerontological social workers should be knowledgeable about alcohol abuse and older adults, and about treatment resources in local communities. Thus, when a clergyman or -woman contacts a social worker, the worker conducts a comprehensive assessment of the client's problem and plans for a referral of the client and family to an appropriate treatment facility.

QUESTIONS FOR DISCUSSION: CASE 1

1. What is the social worker's primary task in this case?
2. What is the role of the minister?
3. How should the social worker involve the daughter?
4. What other information should the social worker have about the client before completing the assessment?

CASE 2: A COMMUNITY IN NEED OF A RESPITE PROGRAM

The second case illustrates the role of social workers as program planners for religious organizations.

The rabbi in the local synagogue has heard from several members of the congregation that caregivers for older persons with Alzheimer's disease in his community need help. The rabbi would like to explore some ideas for programs for caregivers and contacts a social worker.

INTERVIEW: CASE 2

Social worker: I appreciate that you called me to discuss a new program for this community.

Rabbi Strasser: The families of some of my members are suffering with the burden of caring for mothers, fathers, spouses, sisters, and brothers with dementia and other physical and mental problems.

Social worker: Respite programs have been reported to be of help to family members to provide some relief from the daily care of a frail older family member.

Rabbi Strasser: How do we start such a program?

Social worker: First, we must do a needs assessment to determine the extent of the community need for a respite program.

Rabbi Strasser: How can we make it work?

Social worker: If there is a need, collaborative efforts by synagogue members and other members of the community will be essential.

Rabbi Strasser: Who should we contact?

Social worker: It is crucial to call a meeting of interested persons to begin to focus on the needs expressed by the community. Then, we can plan regular meetings and decide on an agenda. We can set a timetable—when we would like this program to begin—and outline the steps necessary for implementation.

Rabbi Strasser: Who should we ask for help?

Social worker: Most religious congregations have many professionals as members. We can involve experts from the membership, such as lawyers, physicians, psychiatrists, nurses, social workers, business leaders, agency directors, and so on.

Rabbi Strasser: Where will we house the program? How much will it cost?

Social worker: These questions will be answered at a later time.

COMMENTS ON CASE 2

Case 2 illustrates macro-level community work in a religious environment. Social workers are trained in program development, needs assessment, social action, and community planning. "Macro social work practice is the practice of solving social problems and making social change at the community, organizational or societal levels" (Brueggemann, 1996. p. 3). Macro-level social workers apply skills such as needs assessment when communities have social problems to resolve. The first step is to determine the needs of the community: for example, How many caregivers are there in the community? Are there resources to pay for a respite center? Can there be federal or local funding for startup costs? Community planning involves a problem-solving process that explores conditions causing social problems. A rational problem-solving process is often used in macro social work. Its components are (p. 57):

1. Deciding on a problem
2. Gathering information about the problem
3. Generating a number of alternative solutions
4. Assessing and comparing alternatives
5. Selecting the best or most cost-beneficial solution
6. Developing a strategy or plan of implementation
7. Carrying out or implementing the solution
8. Evaluating the results.

The macro-level social work practitioner trained in gerontology is well qualified to help a religious organization develop programs and services for older adults. In case 2, the gerontological social worker will use the skills of needs assessment, rational problem solving, and collaboration to bring together community professionals to develop a program for caregivers. The synagogue is the vehicle for the provision of this service. When the group is assembled, the social worker will use small-group skills such as contracting for a purpose of the meetings, setting a time frame for implementation of the program, and developing goals for the group to achieve. The social worker will also use small-group skills such as describing purposes and functions, balancing "task needs" and emotional needs, developing goals, and setting a structure for the work. The social worker will also use macro-level skills such as marketing, public relations, fund raising, and even grant writing in this case. Social work in a religious setting can be both micro-level or macro-level practice.

QUESTIONS FOR DISCUSSION: CASE 2

1. Why is it necessary to conduct a needs assessment?
2. What agencies and individuals should contribute to the needs assessment?
3. What specialized knowledge does the social worker need to be effective?
4. What is the task of the religious leader?
5. How does this task relate to the social work task?

CASE 3: THE 100-YEAR-OLD AUNT

The third case illustrates an ethical dilemma for a church leader and a family—and the social work tasks of mediation and advocacy.

> Madeline Louis is 100 years old. She was never married. She has heart disease, arthritis, and diabetes. A month ago she had a heart attack. She returned home and now has hospice care. Two nieces, Rena and Joan, live next-door. Madeline is being tube-fed, has decubitus (pressure) ulcers, sleeps on a vibrating water bed, is suctioned several times a day, has a catheter, and does not respond to any verbal stimuli. One niece, Rena, asks the doctor to remove all life sustaining equipment. Another niece, Joan, feels that the aunt will die when God is ready for her. A priest is called to help resolve the conflict for this Catholic family.

Rena: Father, I believe Aunt Madeline has suffered enough and we should ask the doctor to remove all life-sustaining equipment for her.
Joan: Father, I believe that she will die when God is ready for her, and that we should not hasten her death.
Priest: Did she leave any written plans?
Rena: No, but she had told me that she did not want life support.
Priest: I believe that we need someone to mediate this conflict for us. We cannot accept the decision of either of you. We can discuss this dilemma with the hospice social worker.

COMMENTS ON CASE 3

Case 3 illustrates the task of the gerontological social worker in advocating for a client who is no longer able to express her own wishes. The social worker will also act as a mediator for the family. In this case, specialized

knowledge of the hospice program and collaboration with the multidisciplinary team are essential for resolution of the conflict. The social worker
will bring together various professionals (such as an "elder lawyer" and the
priest) to consider the patient's options. The function of the agency (the
church) is to give spiritual support to the family and define religious law.
The social worker serves as a mediator for the family but is primarily guided
by the legal principle of consent. This principle, which derives from the
constitutional right of privacy, guarantees the right of a competent individual to make choices for himself or herself, including decisions about
health care. A person can be declared incompetent only in a court of law. If
Madeline Louis had authorized a health care proxy or completed a living
will, the dilemma might have been avoidable. Under the present circumstances, the only legal recourse is to bring the case to court. The social
worker acts as an advocate for the client. In any potential conflict among
church, individual, and family, the social worker acts as mediator in accor-
dance with Madeline's rights. It is a primary tenet of social work practice
that the interest of the client overrides all others.

QUESTIONS FOR DISCUSSION: CASE 3

1. Who should make the decision to withdraw life-sustaining equipment?

2. What are the conflicts of values underlying the issue?

3. How does the social worker mediate in the conflict of values?

4. What specialized knowledge of the religious environment is necessary?

5. Although, in this case, the church and the law are not in conflict,
   what are the implications for the social worker's role in a situation
   in which such a conflict may exist (e.g., a request to terminate life
   by lethal injection)?

In chapter 8, we have illustrated social work practice at both the macro and
the micro level. The three cases demonstrate how social work skills are
applied within a functional orientation. Functional social work as an approach to practice emphasizes that the agency's purpose is critical to the
definition of the professional role. An area of potential conflict exists when
two agencies are at cross–purposes in defining the worker's role. The social worker's primary task in such a situation is to mediate in this conflict
between institutional values and tasks. Social work is a profession replete
with values and ethics, including a strong preference for the right of self–
determination. Ethics are standards of behavior in relation to other people.
These standards, which identify what we should do in specific situations,

are based on values or preferences. The social worker must balance personal beliefs with professional beliefs, and must then be prepared to mediate between conflicting values of individuals and organizations. This explains the complexity of interagency collaborative activity, as well as the need for the social worker to be an effective negotiator.

REFERENCES

Abbott, S. D., Garland, D. R., Huffman-Nevins, A., & Stewart, J. B. (1990). Social workers' views of local churches as service providers: Impressions from an exploratory study. *Social Work and Christianity, 17*(1), 7–16.

Brashears, F., & Roberts, M. (1996). The black church as a resource for change. In S.L. Logan (Ed.), *The black family,* (pp.181–193). Boulder, CO: Westview.

Brueggemann, W.G. (1996). *The practice of macro social work.* Chicago: Nelson-Hall.

Doka, K. J. (1986). The church and the elderly: The impact of changing age stata on congregations. *International Journal of Aging and Human Development, 22*(4), 291–300.

Filinson, R. (1988). A model for church-based services for frail elderly persons and their families. *The Gerontologist, 28*(4). 483–486.

Hooyman, N., & Kiyak, H.A. (1993). *Social gerontology.* (3rd. ed.). Boston: Allyn and Bacon.

Logan, S. L. (ed.) (1996). *The black family.* Boulder, CO: Westview, pp. 181–193.

Moberg, D.O. (1991). Preparing for the graying of the church. *Review and Expositor, 88,* 179–192.

Osgood, N. J., Wood, H., & Parham, I. A. (1995). *Alcoholism and aging: An annotated bibliography and review.* Westport, CT: Greenwood.

Penrod, Joan D., Kane, Rosalie, Kane, Robert, & Finch, Michael. (1995). Who cares? The size, scope and composition of the caregiver support system. *The Gerontologist, 35, 4,* 489–498.

Popple, P. R., & Leighninger, L. (1996). *Social work, social welfare, and American society* (3rd ed.) pp. 138–140. Boston: Allyn and Bacon.

Statistical abstracts of the United States. (111th ed.) (1993). Washington, DC: U.S. Government Printing Office.

Taylor, R.J. (1993). Religion and religious observances. In J. Jackson, L. Chatters, & R. Taylor (Eds.), *Aging in black America* (pp. 101–123). Newbury Park, CA: Sage.

Tobin, S. S., Ellor, J. W., & Anderson-Ray, S. (1986). *Enabling the elderly: Religious institutions within the community service system.* Albany: State University of New York Press.

CHAPTER 9

Gerontological Social Work Practice in a Work Environment

INTRODUCTION

Work influences life in many ways. Demographic trends are affecting work patterns now and will continue to do so well into the next century. Work patterns that reflect the increased longevity of men and women are emerging. Both men and women are working longer and spending more years in retirement than at any other time in our history. Jobs are affecting older workers, and older workers are affecting jobs. In the United States, a male born in 1900 had a life expectancy of 47 years, which meant that he would work for 32 years (70 percent of his lifetime) and be retired for about 1 year (6 percent of his lifetime). Current labor market trends indicate that a male born in 1987 could live about 75 years, work about 55 percent of his lifetime, and be retired for about 20 percent of his lifetime. A female born in 1900 had a life expectancy of 48 years and could expect to spend 6 years (30 percent) of her life in the labor force after childbearing and child rearing. A female born in 1987 can expect to spend at least 40 percent of her 78-year life span in the work force (Hooyman & Kiyak, 1993, p. 359). Americans are now leaving work in their early sixties and looking forward to 20 or 30 years of retirement.

Labor statistics indicate that among people over age 65, only 17 percent of men and 8 percent of women are in the labor force (AARP, 1990). Older workers account for only 3 percent of the total work force, and they are less likely to be in jobs that are physically demanding or "high-tech." But the trend toward early retirement from full-time employment has increased, the trend toward part-time work has also increased—to over 50 percent of retired workers (Barrow, 1996). The current pattern in retirement is a result of affordability of retirement, individual desires, and social acceptance of retirement (Sandell, 1994). The trend is for older men to favor retirement while older women are entering or remaining in the workforce (Barrow, 1996).

Hooyman and Kiyak write:

> Economic status in old age is largely influenced by environmental conditions, especially past and current employment patterns and resulting retirement benefits. For many people, economic status is consistent across the life course. For example, ethnic minorities in low-paying jobs in young and middle adulthood generally face a continuation of poverty in old age. Other older people, including widowed or divorced women who depended on their husbands' income, or retirees with only Social Security as income, may face poverty or near-poverty for the first time in their lives. (1996, p. 358)

It is predicted that there will be a need for new opportunities for older workers in the next century since a majority of the older population are likely to seek employment, owing to increased longevity, a better educated cohort, a healthier cohort of older persons, and economic expectations (people expect to maintain their lifestyle)—as well as the high cost of health care and long term care (Hooyman & Kiyak, 1996).

PROBLEMS IN EMPLOYMENT OF OLDER PERSONS

Gelfand (1993) writes that "the problem of employment for the elderly is twofold: (1) finding employers who did not discriminate against them; (2) finding sufficient numbers of part-time jobs which provide additional money without exceeding the limit allowed by Social Security regulations" (p.126). Thus it seems that ageism, age discrimination, and finding part-time or full-time jobs are major problems for older adults.

Age discrimination refers to denying employment or promotion to someone on the basis of age (Cavanugh, 1996). The Age Discrimination Employment Act of 1967 outlawed discrimination based on age. The original act covered employees between ages 40 and 65. In 1978, it was amended to include people up to age 70. The act (as amended in 1978) prohibits the following:

1. Failing to hire a worker between age 40 and 70 because of age.

2. Discharging a person because of age.

3. Discrimination in pay or other benefits because of age.

4. Limiting or classifying an employee according to his or her age.

5. Instructing an employment agency not to refer a person to a job because of age, or to refer a person only to certain kinds of jobs because of age.

6. Placing any ad that shows preference based on age or specifies an age bracket.

Exceptions are: the federal government, employers of less than 20 persons, and jobs where youth is a "bona fide occupational qualification," such as modeling teenage clothes (Barrow, 1996, p. 157).

In 1986, 1.1 million workers were over the age of 70, and it is estimated that 195,000 more older workers will join the labor force by the year 2000 (Gelfand, 1993). Employment programs are beginning to address the needs of older workers and are offering part-time work and retraining to acquire new skills.

However, unemployment is rising among older workers as a result of plant closings, downsizing, and restructuring. When older workers are unemployed, they tend to stay out of work longer, and experience a greater loss in earnings, and they are more likely to become discouraged and stop looking for work (Hooyman & Kiyak, 1996). Early retirement has become common in both the white-collar world and the blue-collar world, and many companies offer early retirement plans. In fact, some companies are being accused of discrimination in this regard: (Barrow, 1996) that is, they have induced or forced the retirement of older workers. When incentives for early retirement are offered to employees, very often the retirement is not voluntary; for example, a worker will be fired or transferred to a less desirable position if the offer is not accepted.

Negative views of aging contribute to loss of jobs for older persons. Business leaders continue to see the consumer market as young in spite of the fact that in 1990 the median age of Americans was 31 years, and it is projected to be 37 years in 2020 (U.S. Census Bureau, 1993). Business in America looks for young people to interact in the corporate world. Age discrimination may even start when people are in their thirties—people of that age may not be accepted for flight school or medical school, for instance (Barrow, 1996).

Changes in the labor market are creating a new work environment. The trend toward downsizing is creating situations in which part-time employees are preferred. Thus, older, retired workers can be an asset to an employer if they can afford to accept part-time work without benefits.

Although many older workers would like to work part-time in new jobs, their skills and talents often go unused because little part-time work is available to them and Social Security limits the amount of money an older worker can earn without losing benefits. Other barriers to the employment of older adults are a poor work history, a long lag period since their last job, and inappropriate skills for a changing, technology-oriented labor market (Gelfand, 1993). Physical problems such as chronic illnesses (like arthritis and heart disease), or functional limitations (such as difficulty walking and inability to lift), and emotional problems may also hinder the older person's job search.

Some federal programs train older workers. One of these programs is the Senior Community Service Employment Program (SCSEP), which is supported by Title V of the Older Americans Act. A number of major organizations nationwide have been contracted by the Department of Labor to administer this program on the local level, and in 1990 the program had a budget of $367 million (Gelfand, 1993). Funds are distributed through various local organizations to train persons over age 55 who meet economic eligibility criteria. These older adults are then placed in jobs that provide community services. The majority of SCSEP participants are women, some of them minority elderly women. Thirty percent are over age 70. The majority are in their sixties, though, and the rest are 55 to 60 years of age. There are some problems with SCSEP: its goals often conflict with the realities of the job market for older adults, and in its current form the program creates a dependency situation for the employer and employee. The Job Partnership Training Act (JPTA), which replaced the Community Employment Training Act (CETA), designates 3% of its funds for poorer workers over 55. The JPTA provides training and remedial education as well as counseling and assistance in looking for jobs.

Older persons have difficulty in finding new jobs because of age discrimination in the workplace, lack of new skills (e.g., computer literacy), ageist social policies (limits on earned income for Social Security recipients), and myths about older workers. There are several common myths about older workers:

Myth: Older workers cannot produce as much as younger workers.

Myth: Older workers lack physical strength and endurance.

Myth: Older workers are set in their ways.

Myth: Older workers do not mix well with younger workers—they tend to be grouchy.

Myth: Older workers are difficult to train—they learn slowly.

Myth: Older workers lack drive and imagination—they cannot project an enthusiastic, aggressive image. (Barrow, 1996, p.161)

Along with a changing labor market, these myths are a major barrier to the employment of older persons. However, such attitudes are expected to change as the population ages and the baby boomers become a major factor in on the workforce.

WHAT IS SOCIAL WORK PRACTICE
IN THE WORK ENVIRONMENT?

Social workers can be employed in a variety of positions in a work environment. They function as management consultants, trainers, program planners, program evaluators, administrators, managers, supervisors, fund raisers, marketing and public relations employees, occupational and industrial social workers, and "employee assistance persons" (EAPs).

To sum up, problems in the employment of older persons are attributable to:

- Age discrimniation
- Lack of part-time work
- Lack of new skills
- Ageism

Occupational social workers are often referred to as EAP social workers. They perform a variety of tasks in an organization, such as counseling, referral services, and studies of the work environment. Employees with alcohol or drug abuse problems are referred to an EAP social worker for counseling or referral to community agencies. EAP social workers also develop programs at work sites, such as day care programs for children of employees. Mediation and advocacy (e.g., discrimination cases) are also tasks of an occupational social worker or EAP. A current issue in the workplace is cultural sensitivity, and corporations are implementing sensitivity training programs for employees at all levels of the organization. These training sessions are often conducted by occupational social workers. Federal and state agencies also hire social workers in employee assistance programs.

Social work practice has been described as "the doing of social work" (Kirst-Ashman & Hull, 1993, p. 10). They state "it involves how to form relationships with clients, help them to share information with you, identify and evaluate numerous alternatives for action, make specific plans, implement these plans.... The social work knowledge base includes knowledge of skills in addition to knowledge of problems and services. A social worker must know which skills will be most effective in which situation." In a generalist framework, social workers are not experts in only casework, group work, or community organization. Generalist practice sees social workers as having a base of skills which can be used for micro or macro levels of practice.

THE WORKERS' ROLES

Both micro- and macro-level social work practice can be found in the work environment. Macro-level social work practice involves working for solutions to social problems and creating social change. It encompasses community social work, organizational social work, and societal social work. Macro-level social workers are social activists, social planners, program developers, administrators, and community organizers. Methodology in the workplace can be casework, group work, administration, or community organization. The gerontological social worker adds knowledge of biopsychosocial aspects of aging and knowledge of the specialized setting to social work practice in a work environment.

At the micro level, in public agencies or private corporations social workers counsel employees and their families, lead groups, and become involved in community work. Social workers counsel employees who have martial problems, alcohol and drug problems, or problems with caregiving and child care. The social worker may be called upon to mediate in a conflict between coworkers or between a worker and supervisor. Group work skills may be used in training programs for resolving employee-versus-management issues. Training sessions in conflict resolution, teamwork, or communication can be effective in resolving conflicts between management and employees. In the nonprofit sector the social worker needs to know how to work with boards, raise funds, and prepare marketing and public relations plans.

In the following case the social worker uses knowledge of issues of aging and knowledge of a specialized setting to help the client. The principle of generalist social work practice primarily illustrated is assessment.

CASE EXAMPLE 1:
EMPLOYEE WITH AN ALCOHOL PROBLEM

Cathy C., age 60, widow, is a full-time employee of a university. She is a secretary. She has been in this position for four months. Her responsibilities include typing, answering the telephone, and being the front-office receptionist. She has a pleasant personality and is congenial and polite. Her work is satisfactory. However, she is absent frequently (once or twice a month) and has been seen asleep at her desk. She sometimes seems dazed, and sometimes she has a scent of alcohol. She is referred to the employee assistance worker in the human resources department.

INTERVIEW: CASE 1

Social Worker: Cathy, you have been referred to this office to discuss a work-related problem. The supervisor of your department is very concerned about your absenteeism and reports that you have been seen sleeping at your desk.

Cathy: I have been having trouble sleeping at night and then become awfully sleepy during the day. Some nights I can't fall asleep until the early morning hours, and then I have trouble waking up.

Social worker: Has anything changed recently that is affecting your sleep?

Cathy: Well, my husband, John, died last year. We had been married for 40 years. My daughter, Angela, lives in New York and my son, Bob, lives in Charleston. I have worked for the university for 10 years in various positions as a floater. I really enjoy my work. When my husband was living, we were very busy visiting the children, going to the movies, and having dinner with friends. Now I don't do very much. I watch television and read and sometimes crochet. I love my job. I get to meet and talk to people all day, but when I get home, it's lonely.

Social worker: What happens when you feel lonely?

Cathy: Not too much. I just turn on the TV and feel depressed. I start to think about John, and I miss him.

Social worker: When you have trouble falling asleep, do you take something to help you sleep?

Cathy: No, I don't believe in taking pills.

Social worker: What about a glass of wine?

Cathy: Yes, I enjoy wine. It helps to relax me and I hear that it lowers blood pressure.

Social worker: So, you're also feeling anxious as well as depressed?

Cathy: I get scared about the future.

COMMENTS ON CASE 1

In case 1 the social worker uses an assessment tool (Multidisciplinary Screening Instrument; see Appendix) to provide a comprehensive assessment of the client's functioning. From the assessment, the social worker determines that Cathy may be having a problem with alcohol abuse. The social worker, who is knowledgeable about alcoholism, and about alcohol abuse among older adults, knows that older persons often do not admit that drinking several glasses of wine at dinner or a brandy after dinner can become problematic for them. The social worker makes an assessment that this is a case of late-onset alcohol abuse and recommends treatment at a program that specializes in the treatment of older adults. Age-specific treatment programs have been found to have high rates of success in the treatment of late-onset substance abuse in older adults (Osgood, Wood, & Parham, 1995).

QUESTIONS FOR DISCUSSION : CASE 1

1. What other questions should the social worker ask to provide a comprehensive assessment of the client's needs?
2. What other types of resources might be available to help the client?
3. If the client is part of a representative group of employees with similar problems, is there anything that the organization could provide to help individuals with such problems (e.g., isolation and bereavement)?

CASE EXAMPLE 2: AGE DISCRIMINATION IN A HOSPITAL

In case 2, the social worker mediates between the employee and the administration.

> Phyliss M., age 65, works for Mercy Hospital as a clerk in the radiology department. She has been a part-time, temporary employee for 3 years. The department manager will not hire her as a permanent employee. Phyliss was placed at Mercy Hospital by the Senior Community Service Employment Program (SCSEP). She was assigned to this position for 6 months but has remained for 3 years. Phyliss was retrained by the SCSEP to use a computer and word processor. Her evaluations are excellent, and she is well liked by her coworkers. Phyliss has an excellent attendance record. She manages the files for the department, and handles all appointments, mail, meeting schedules, and payments by clients. As a part-time employee, she is not entitled to vacation time, sick time, or health benefits. Fortunately, though, she is enrolled in the Medicare program. In the interviews below, Phyliss meets with the hospital employment assistance counselor (social worker).

Phyliss: I came to see you because I think the department manager will not hire me as a permanent employee. I think the hospital is discriminating against me because I am an older person . I've worked in this department for 3 years. New employees are hired all the time. I want to have the benefits of a permanent employee. I have asked my manager to hire me as a full-time worker, I'm told that the hospital does not have funds for me.

Social worker: Have you discussed your situation with the department manager?

Phyliss: Yes, I am told that a permanent position is not available . However, as I told you, new permanent employees have been hired in the last 3 years. I've heard they are afraid to hire older persons because they think we will cost too much in health care benefits. I never miss a day. I'm in good health. I am never late, though I have to take three buses to get to work.

Social worker: What are your assignments?

Phyliss: I manage the files and make all the appointments for the X-ray department. I work part-time, 9 a.m. to 3 p.m. and the bulk of the work is completed during that time. I know that they don't have any older people working here, and I hear remarks about why I don't stay home and enjoy life. I like my work, and I enjoy having a job. I like to feel that I have something important to do. Being old is very difficult in today's society. You seem to be in the way and are given little respect.

Social worker: When you were assigned to this position by the SCSEP, was it a temporary position?

Phyliss: Yes, it was. However, it was understood that I could be hired as a permanent employee when I finished the computer training. I have done very well with the computer, and I enjoy my work. However, I need some benefits from this job, such as paid vacation. My only other source of income is a pension check from Social Security which my husband earned. I was a homemaker for 30 years. I have no retirement income of my own, and I have a very small income. I currently earn the minimum wage, with little hope of earning more. I am having a very difficult time financially. If I don t work for a few days, I don't get paid. It is very difficult to live on this limited income, and I am worried about my future. How will I pay my bills?

COMMENTS ON CASE 2

In case 2 the social worker must have knowledge of the setting (the hospital), the law (Age Discrimination Act of 1967), the SCSEP program, and issues that relate to older women (low income, poor skills, and poor work histories outside of the home). The social worker must know: What are the needs of the hospital? Are there budgetary constraints to hiring Phyliss as a permanent employee? Is the administration taking advantage of older workers? Development of a trusting relationship between the client and the worker is essential.

The social worker makes an assessment of the client to determine her physical, psychological, and social functioning. Is Phyliss able to do the job? To help the client, the social worker must conduct an accurate and comprehensive assessment of the client's situation. The agency's function (or its contract with the client) gives direction and focus to the work. The social worker is an employee of the hospital and must work to resolve the conflict between the institution (the employer) and the client. In this case the social worker must act to mediate between employee and employer and must balance the interests of both.

Another issue in this case has to do with the function of the social worker in relation to the SCSEP program. The SCSEP program was established to retrain older persons in new skills or to train those with poor or no skills for employment. Placement in community agencies was designed as temporary, for the duration of the training period—which was to be short-term. However, many community agencies enjoyed the benefits of free labor and were reluctant to hire the trainees after the training period. Some trainees became entrenched in the community agency and did not seek employment in other agencies. The program's original mission—short-term training of older workers in a community agency —was no longer its focus. Some older workers had remained in training for 1 to 7 years. The social worker in this case can be an advocate for social change in a program that is not meeting its goals and is instead creating dependency and conflict for agencies and older workers.

QUESTIONS FOR DISCUSSION: CASE 2

1. How are the tasks of the social worker determined by the agency's function?
2. What is the social worker's responsibility to the hospital?
3. What ethical dilemmas are involved in this case?
4. What should the social worker's focus be with the SCSEP program?
5. Why is it necessary to have a comprehensive assessment of the client in this case?
6. What strategies might you use to achieve change in this situation?

The following cases illustrate two recent trends in corporations: (1) to force the older worker to leave the job, and (2) to use older persons in the part-time work force.

CASE EXAMPLE 3: FORCED RETIREMENT

Victor T., retired from a major computer corporation at age 60 with an excellent retirement package. In the last 2 years at work, he had been excluded from travel to conferences and from attending major corporate meetings. At that time, he was offered 1 year's salary ($60,000), stock options, and a pension ($5,000 a month) based on his last 3 years of earnings. However, after 5 years when he was 65, he became eligible to collect a monthly Social Security pension of $1,000. Thereafter, his corporate pension was then reduced to $1,000 monthly, so that he now had a monthly income of $2,000—which is annually $24,000. He does have some income from corporate stocks—$1,000 monthly—making his total income $36,000. When he became eligible for Medicare, his corporate health benefits were reduced; thus Medicare became his primary insurer. He is the sole supporter of his family. His wife did not work outside of the home.

QUESTIONS FOR DISCUSSION: CASE 3

1. Is the company being fair to the employee by reducing his medical benefits when he reaches age 65?
2. Did the company force Victor to retire or provide an incentive for retirement?
3. Did Victor have a choice?
4. What other options could have been made available to Victor?
5. Is this case an example of age discrimination?
6. What strategies would you employ to help Victor or other employees to secure their rights?

CASE EXAMPLE 4: PART-TIME EMPLOYEE

Marilyn A., age 58 , widow, is a part-time employee for a temporary clerical agency. She does word processing and general clerical duties. She has no benefits such as vacation time, sick time, or health insurance. She earns the minimum wage. She is unable to find a full-time job. She is not eligible for Social Security benefits, but she is fortunate to have her deceased husband's pension annuity. She helps her 22-year-old son who is finishing college. She is depressed over her future. She meets with the EAP worker of the agency to ask for help. The social worker makes a complete assessment of her biopsychosocial functioning. Her apparent depression is related to her economic situation and her loss of self-esteem.

COMMENTS ON CASES 3 AND 4

In case examples 3 and 4, the social worker is dealing with older workers who are facing problems in the work environment due to age discrimination. Several methods of intervention are used:

1. Assessment and diagnosis of the clients

2. Mediation and negotiation with the administration of the organization

3. Advocacy for social change regarding the laws on retirement incentives, and the laws on benefits to part-time workers

4. Counseling and referral for treatment of depression as it relates to the work environment.

Several practice methods can be applied in these settings. One of these is group work. Group sessions can help employees prepare for retirement by making them aware of their options at work and their increased needs as they age. Social workers advocate employee's empowerment or enable employees to empower themselves, and they can also advocate protective legislation. Changes in social policy require social action. Laws are needed to protect the older worker, and gerontological social workers are in a good position to work toward social change. However, a social worker in an organizational setting must balance the needs of the organization with those of the employee. Therefore, efforts must be made to demonstrate the cost-effectiveness of retaining older employees, or providing options for part-time work. The use of part-time personnel is expected to increase as companies downsize and offer more flexible scheduling for employees in an effort to recruit traditionally underrepresented groups (older workers, minorities, and women; Ewalt, 1993). This development is a response to a decreasing labor market in service positions. Although the trend is a mixed blessing for underrepresented workers, it at least provides some impetus for growth in part-time employment opportunities.

Marilyn, the part-time employee (case 4), is suffering from psychological symptoms precipitated by a social issue. A historical tenet of social work practice is that the social environment contributes to the individual's mental and physical health. The focus of systems theory is that the individual is affected by many systems, and the work environment is one of these systems.

Gerontological social work practice, as we describe it, is the integration of principles of general practice with specialized knowledge of issues of aging and knowledge of specific settings of practice. Each of the cases in this chapter illustrates a different work setting and a different problem. The social worker's knowledge of the setting is essential for effective practice. The agency (organization or business) determines the social worker's role according to the function of the agency. In other words, the social worker must not forget who the employer is but must also consider the client's need for service. The social worker's specialized knowledge of issues of aging (e.g., depression and alcohol abuse) helps in planning for effective service for the older adult. Gerontological social work practice in the work environment can be with individuals, groups, communities, or organizations. Roles are both micro and macro: they include counseling, group leadership, administration, negotiating, mediating, planning, using political skills, and working for social justice. We would like to emphasize what has been stated earlier in this book: we support the view that the best social work incorporates micro activities (with individuals and small groups) as well as macro activities (with organizations and the community). We believe that gerontological social work practice in the work environment will become a major field in the next decade.

REFERENCES

American Association of Retired Persons (AARP). *A profile of older Americans.* (1990). Washington, DC: AARP

Barrow, G. M. 1996. *Aging, the individual, society.* (6th ed.) Minneapolis/St. Paul: West.

Cavanaugh, J. (1996). *Adult development and aging.* (3rd ed.) Pacific Grove, CA: Brooks/Cole.

Ewalt, P. (1991). *Trends affecting recruitment and retention of social work staff in human service agencies. Social Work, 36,* 3.

Gelfand, Donald (1993). *The aging network: programs and services* (4th ed.) New York: Springer.

Hooyman, N., & Kiyak, A. (1996). *Social gerontology* (4th ed.). Boston: Allyn and Bacon.

Kirst-Ashman, K. K. & Hull, G. H (1993). *Understanding generalist practice.* Chicago: Nelson-Hall.

Osgood, N.J., Wood, H., & Parham, I. (1995). *Alcoholism and aging: An annotated bibliography and review.* Westport, CT: Greenwood.

Sandell, S. (1994). In R. Moody, *Aging: Controversies and issues,* Thousand Oaks, CA: Pine Forge.

U.S. Census Bureau. (1990). *Statistical abstracts: 1993.* Washington, DC: U.S. Government Printing Office.

CHAPTER 10

Gerontological Social Work Practice in a Political Environment

---

INTRODUCTION

What is gerontological social work practice in a political environment? In this chapter, *political environment* refers to an arena for social change. It is in the law, in the community, and in the organization that social change takes place. Social change is necessary to enhance quality of life for everyone. Social change solves social problems, and social workers are a vital force in solving social problems. How to solve social problems is the focus of social work practice. Social work practice is based on helping "the person in the environment." It is a tenet of social work practice that the environment influences the client's well-being and problems. A comprehensive assessment of the client's environment includes determining the factors that affect his or her situation and planning interventions to improve his or her life.

Thus in this chapter *social work practice in a political environment* refers to the social worker's role as an advocate for changing laws and policies, as a community organizer helping communities to solve social problems, and as an administrator in an organization developing programs and promoting social change. Solving social problems, advocacy, community organizing, program development, and administrative work are all activities of gerontological social work in the political setting.

SOCIAL CHANGE AND SOCIAL PROBLEMS

Social workers are agents of change who strive to solve social problems. Brueggemann (1996) writes, "Social workers see communities, organizations and society as the arenas of their concern and involvement"(p. 4). Social workers are involved in policy decisions and make social changes by advocating changes in public and social policies. Brueggemann describes public policies as "operating principles by which governmental systems carry out their goals," and social policies as "operating premises developed to provide direction in the solution of social problems" (p. 345).

Social policies have an impact on the lives of many older adults. Changes in Medicare laws affect access to health care services for millions of older persons. For example, since Medicare does not pay for dentures, older persons who need them but are unable to pay for them may be toothless. Medicare regulations determine how much doctors and hospitals are reimbursed for an older person's care. Medicare regulations decide how many days a person can be treated in a hospital setting. Changes in these regulations had a major impact on the health care of older persons in the 1980s and again in the 1990s because the method of payment to hospitals was changed from retrospective to prospective. Hospitals reduced the length of stay for older persons and sent them home sooner and sicker.

Reimbursement policies for home care have a major influence on the services provided by home care agencies to older adults nationwide, because the number of hours of services, and the types of services, (e.g, social workers, housekeepers, and nutritionists) are monitored by state and federal agencies.

Prior to 1990 nursing homes were using physical and chemical restraints to control patients' behavior. Changes in the law were necessary to allow older persons to be free of restraints in nursing homes. In 1990 the Omnibus Reconciliation Act required nursing homes to keep their patients as free of restraints as possible. The law required nursing home physicians to justify the use of physical and chemical restraints through team evaluations.

New laws are needed to protect older persons in independent living centers. Currently there is little or no regulation, since these facilities are not under Medicare or Medicaid guidelines. Thus, there is often little supervision, there may be arbitrary rules for transfer and discharge, and there may be few regulated admission procedures and little interest in enforcing the Patient's Bill of Rights required in more regulated nursing homes (personal communication, 1996).

Another example of the laws to solve social problems is the Age Discrimination Act, which prohibits discrimination in the workplace. This law was a major impetus in allowing older persons to remain in the workforce until they want to retire.

ADVOCACY

Advocacy is vital in public and private social service agencies, because community social service agencies are competing for scarce, limited resources in a conservative political climate. In the 1960s the social work profession enjoyed a time of abundant social programs; but in the 1970s the ideology of social welfare changed, and federal and state spending on social programs came under increasing scrutiny. In the 1980s a strongly conservative political climate developed, which is still evident in the 1990s. Scarce resources, poor services, and a distrust of the political process are becoming characteristic of many communities. The social worker's role as advocate is even more vital in this political climate.

Social workers must learn to be advocates for their clients, with a renewed emphasis on community organization, planning, and policy making. Social workers are involved in strategic planning, legal problems, advocacy issues, mediation, and policy making as well as the traditional methods: casework, group work, and administration.

Social change involves advocating a better life for older adults. In 1965 major legislation for older persons was enacted—the Medicare and Medicaid Acts. In 1965 the Older Americans Act provided funds to states for services, training, and research to help older persons. In 1981, Title V, which had first been activated in 1973, added funding for multipurpose centers, and the senior center became the focus of delivery of services. The Administration on Aging is authorized to make grants to states for the construction, acquisition, and renovation of buildings to be used as senior centers. In 1978, the Older Americans Act funded "congregate meals" sites and home-delivered meals. Other programs established by the Older Americans Act were employment programs, transportation programs, legal services, and geriatric training and research projects. The White House Conferences on Aging in 1970 and 1980 helped to improve the lives of older adults in America by providing for senior employment programs, the building of senior centers in every state and in almost every county, nutrition programs and recreation programs. In 1995, at the White House Conference on Aging, older persons presented a list of concerns—areas in which change was needed in order to improve their social, financial, and environmental conditions. In the coming years continued and strong legislative advocacy will be needed to help solve the problems of older persons in this country.

COMMUNITY ORGANIZING

Social workers traditionally were community organizers. Early community organization took place in New York City and Chicago, where settlement houses helped to improve living conditions for newly arrived immigrants in the early 1900s. The Charity Organization Movement was a grassroots effort that established neighborhood centers and provided a variety of services for adults and children. These efforts were an early form of community social work practice. Community organization was the domain of social work. Community action groups were organized by social workers who demanded changes in the living and working conditions of children and adults in this country. Community organization continues today in rural and urban areas, where social workers help organize neighborhood coalitions to make neighborhoods safe from crime, develop new organizations to solve social problems. Social workers are a vital force in private as well as public institutions that help the poor, the homeless, the sick, and the old.

When an older person is frail and isolated in a rural area, health care services are often not available. Some older persons in rural areas live in deteriorating houses. Communities are trying to help. Community organizing has been effective in solving some of these problems in rural areas. In urban areas, where crime against older persons is a serious problem, bringing together coalitions of public and private organizations has helped reduce such crime.

Gerontological social workers can have a vital role as advocates when they bring older adults together in groups and empower them to help themselves. Group methods are most effective in teaching older adults to empower themselves, but the use of these methods with older adults for the purpose of social action is a relatively new strategy. Group work with older adults requires the specialized skills and knowledge of the gerontologically trained social worker. It is essential to be knowledgeable about issues of aging. New programs and services, prevention of crime, advocacy for victims, adult protective services, senior housing, and recreational facilities are just a few of the areas for political and community action. Group work as a social work method with community groups is discussed in one of the case examples in this chapter.

Community organization and community action programs may be seen as actions by the social work profession to move agencies to meet the needs of the poor. Welfare departments, landlords, housing authorities, and schools were not meeting the needs of the poor in the community, and in the 1960s antipoverty programs were designed to force these agencies to change. Today's community action groups are involved in crime prevention, racial issues, environmental waste control, prevention of uncontrolled expansion and development, school problems, and any other community problems for which there has been no response from government. Community action groups work for social change. Community action groups work to resolve issues that threaten the well-being of a community or specific groups of its members. For example, in a suburb of a large city some seniors are unable to make needed repairs on their homes, and teenagers from the local high school collect supplies donated from businesses in the area and make the needed repairs.

PROGRAM DEVELOPMENT

Another area of social work practice is program development. The following are some programs for older adults which need to be changed or developed.

- *Meals-on-Wheels:* In this program, local communities provide a (usually) daily meal to older homebound people. In some states there are long waiting lists for this program. In one state, 700 people are on the waiting list (personal communication, 1996). Changes in eligibility requirements would allow more people to receive meals each day. Another problematic issue for Meals-on-Wheels is that meals are delivered only on weekdays. It seems reasonable to assume that an older person who needs a daily meal would also need a meal on weekends.

- *Adult day care programs in local hospitals:* Local hospitals can provide services that are offered in adult day care programs. For example, day care centers offer medical examinations, prescription checks, physical therapy, and other medical services on their premises. It seems relatively easy to have local hospitals combine their services with adult day care programs and even to offer adult day care in the hospital.

- *Respite care programs in adult day care centers:* Adult day care centers for older persons in need of day services or day treatments could easily be used for respite for one day or several days, if funding were available.

- *Hospice care in home care agencies:* Home care agencies provide a variety of services to homebound elderly people, and hospice care could be easily included in this list of services. Duplication of services could be avoided.

- *Local geriatric mental health clinics:* Local community mental health clinics can offer geriatric screening for depression, dementia, alcohol abuse, and other mental disorders of older adults.

- *Elder abuse shelters:* Local communities must provide some shelters specifically for victims of elder abuse. Currently, hospital emergency rooms serve as shelters for older persons.

THE WORKER'S ROLES

Social workers are employed as nursing home administrators, executive directors of home care agencies, administrators of hospice programs, administrators of adult day care centers, administrators of respite programs, supervisors of adult protective services programs, directors of hospital discharge planning units, managers of retirement centers, and directors of state units on aging. The social work administrator has a major impact on the management of a facility. The skills of the social work administrator are vital in bringing to an organization a leader who effectively balances management of employees and the best interests of clients.

Gerontological social workers in the political environment *are community organizers, administrators, advocates,* and *change agents.* Social workers are employed in community agencies as organizers, program planners, grant writers, advocates, strategic planners, administrators, policy makers, public relations persons, fund-raisers, consultants, and other positions that are not traditionally described as social work positions such as quality assurance planners. They are responsible for needs assessments, community liaison work, strategic planning, developing resources, networking, and marketing. The cases later in this chapter will describe the roles of social workers who are community workers, administrators and policy makers.

Social work practice in a political environment involves community organization, advocacy, administration, and promoting social change for the common good. A social worker can be employed in a senior center, a social service agency, a council on aging program, or a state coordinating agency, or even with a legislative body. Social workers have many opportunities to advocate for older adults. For example, social workers who work with Alzheimer's disease organizations advocate for legislation to fund new programs, research, and training for caregivers and service providers. Social workers at the local level develop adult day care programs, respite programs, and educational and leisure programs in their communities.

PRINCIPLES OF GROUP WORK

Group work is an excellent social work method for community organizers involved with older persons. Group work practitioners use skills learned with individuals and apply these skills in a group setting (Schwartz & Zalba, 1971). Group workers' major aims are to distinguish between their own tasks and the tasks of the client (group), to dedicate themselves to the client's need and the service of the agency, to demand that a group adhere to a contract, and to bring the group together to work for a specific purpose.

Schwartz and Zalba (1977, p. 13) state that the tasks of the group worker have four phases. The first is a "tuning-in" phase, in which the worker moves into the group experience as a professional. In the second phase, the worker helps the group to "make its beginnings together." The third phase involves the work that is the specific purpose of the group. The fourth phase is "transitions or endings"—that is, termination.

The five major tasks of the worker are defined as follows by Schwartz and Zalba (p. 16):

1. Finding, through negotiation, a common ground between the requirements of the group members and those of the systems in which they need to navigate
2. Detecting and challenging obstacles to work as such obstacles arise
3. Contributing ideas, facts, and values from his or her own perspective when such data may be useful to the members in dealing with the problems under consideration
4. Lending his or her own vision and projecting his or her own feelings about the struggles in which the group is engaged
5. Defining the requirements and limits of the situation in which the client-worker system is set

Schwartz and Zalba describe group work as different from individual work in that it is a "multiplicity of helping relationships" (p. 17). The group process lends itself particularly well to community work and political advocacy. When group members come together, they share ideas for solving problems, bring more information, and contribute different perspectives. In addition, though, one of the questions confronting social workers in agency settings is noted by Schwartz and Zalba (p. 162): "How does one remain responsive to both the client system and the institutional system, especially when there are elements of conflict between them?"

EFFECTIVE GROUPS

Group methods in themselves are effective change agents. The group is an excellent vehicle for community change. However, the specificity of a group's goals and objectives will determine its success or failure. Homan (1994, p. 300) describes characteristics of effective and ineffective groups. He suggests that effective groups have the following characteristics:

1. Goals are clarified and changed so that the best possible match between individual goals and the group's goals may be achieved.
2. Communication is two-way.
3. Participation and leadership are distributed among all group members.
4. Ability and information determine influence and power.
5. Contracts are built to make sure that individuals' goals and needs are fulfilled.
6. Power is equal and shared.
7. Decision-making procedures are appropriate to the situation.
8. Different methods are used at different times.
9. Consensus is sought for important decisions.
10. Controversy and conflict are seen positively key to members' involvement and the quality and originality of decisions.
11. Interpersonal, group, and intergroup behaviors are stressed.
12. Cohesion is advanced through high levels of inclusion, affection, acceptance, support, and trust.
13. Problem-solving adequacy is highly effective.

14. Members evaluate the effectiveness of the group and decide how to improve its functioning.

15. Interpersonal effectiveness, self-actualization, and innovation are encouraged.

GROUP WORK AND OLDER ADULTS

In the 1970s and 1980s groups with older adults included short-term educational, skill building, reality orientation, remotivation, reminiscence and life review, support, and advocacy. Community action groups usually involve older adults who have the time and energy to work on community problems. Older adults are a valuable resource for this work. They bring to the group ideas from practical experience and perspectives from varied backgrounds. Empowerment in relation to group activities is recognized as the "mutual aid process of the group" (Solomon, 1992. p.112). Solomon describes group activity as:

> one which permits older adults to make social connections, to develop new or retain old skills, to help other members look at issues from another perspective, to negotiate with persons in authority, to develop serviceable strategies for goal accomplishment and to accomplish stated goals.

Group work with older adults must consider the biopsychosocial aspects of aging. The physical changes of the older person must be understood. For example, sensory defects such as hearing loss require others to speak slowly and distinctly. Assessing the energy level of the members is also an important aspect of group work with older adults (Burnside & Schmidt, 1994). It is important for the leader to provide psychological support to increase the group members' confidence and promote cohesiveness. The cognitive level should also be included in assessment of group members. Social aspects include cultural differences, educational differences, socialization, and cohort differences of group members. With regard to cohort differences, for instance, different age groups must be accounted for. Life experiences differ for members who are in their eighties and those members who are in their sixties. Differences in socialization which include upbringing and religion, create cultural differences. Older adults are not homogeneous. It is necessary to consider these factors in the psychosocial assessment of group members.

CASE EXAMPLE 1: A SENIOR CENTER SOCIAL CLUB

In the first case, the executive planning committee of a social club demands that the senior center take a more active position in promoting a community-sponsored crime watch. This case illustrates some of the principles of group work in a community context. It focuses on issues encountered when a client group attempts to redefine its purpose and the social worker needs to mediate between conflicting demands of the client group, the agency, and the community. It also illustrates the importance of psychosocial assessment in understanding group behavior and demonstrates group techniques for promoting a consensus among conflicting demands of a community, an agency and a client group.

Valley Stream Senior Center opened in September 1995 at a cost of $12 million. It had been planned for 12 years and required grassroots organizing, skilled fund-raising, and political advocacy to reach completion. The center began as the dream of five people who petitioned the legislature for funding. The state's revenues from bingo were designated to fund the construction of the senior center. Other fund-raising efforts, such as sales of a cookbook and flowers, produced more money and a public-private effort brought together local businesses and public agencies. Services and time were donated by local architects, construction companies, interior designers, and power companies. Equipment was donated for kitchen facilities, an exercise room, a computer room, and outside areas— a garden, patio, and pool. Social workers are skilled in community work, networking, fund-raising, and advocacy, and several social workers were also involved in this project.

Finally the center opened, with a membership of 1,600 people over age 50. Many activities and programs were planned. One of these was a social club. Other groups were focused on caregiver support and education. Weekly meetings were planned.

The purpose of the social club was clearly defined as socialization. In this group the members planned social activities, including trips, parties for the holidays or other special occasions, dances, and sports events. Within 2 months, however, some of the members demanded that the center take a more active position in promoting a community-sponsored crime watch. The group had to renegotiate its initial purpose for coming together—that is, its contract. It had to redefine its purpose. Was the work of the group to be community action, political activity, or socialization?

The social worker's role as mediator in this conflict was to help the group reach a consensus. The group did reach a consensus: the members wanted to become involved in helping their community. One member stated that it was an opportunity to give something back to the community. Another member said he felt that as retired seniors they had more time and energy to act as advocates for changes in the community than, for instance, young parents, working parents, and young adults, who tend to have more demands on their time. The group agreed that its first project would be a community-sponsored crime watch.

The primary task for the social worker is to understand group behavior and to manage the conflict among the group members. The social worker uses group work methods to manage the tensions of a group experience. In any group certain types usually emerge: a leader, a withdrawn member, a hostile member, a verbal member. It is necessary, in working with groups of older adults to be clearly aware of this tendency It is also necessary to be aware of the cultural and cohort differences of the group members. In particular, older adults may be ambivalent about group work if it has not traditionally been a part of their life experience. For example, some members are from ethnic backgrounds—cultures—that are not verbally expressive. Cohort or educational differences can also account for nonparticipation by some members.

Group techniques can be applied in conflicts to mediate between the community, the agency, and the client group. In this case example, the senior center is supported by many community agencies. The state legislature uses revenues from bingo to fund the center, and several local politicians helped to secure this funding. However, the local politicians are unwilling to support an increase in taxes for more police protection—as are local business and taxpayers.

The executive director and board of directors of the senior center are not pleased with the new direction of the "social club"; they are experiencing some political discomfort, and they are concerned about the center's public image and the possibility that the local community and local business people might withdraw their support. The social worker's task is to mediate between the group, the agency, and the community.

The leader of the group must restate its goals and define the tasks necessary to achieve these goals. The group is interested in developing a crime-watch program for the neighborhood. There are some problems: it is not possible to increase the number of police without raising taxes, seniors are afraid to become involved in nighttime activities because there has been an increase in car theft and robbery in the neighborhood. Still, the plan for a crime watch program seems to be feasible, if the center can collaborate with the local high school and some of the students volunteer to help. Recruitment of volunteers is a major goal. However, before any recruitment activities can be planned, the conflict between the agency (the senior center), the community (the police and community and business leaders), and the client (the group members) must be resolved.

COMMENTS ON CASE EXAMPLE 1

In this case we examine one of the roles of the gerontological social worker as a group worker. We look at issues of change in a group's goals: A group of older adults that began as a social group becomes a social-action group. The social worker mediates between the client group, the agency, and the community. If the group is working within the context of an agency or organization, the goals and objectives of the agency or organization must be kept clear and distinct. If there is conflict, the social worker's task is to redirect the conflict. The worker's task is to clearly state the group's goals and the agency's goals. Sometimes it becomes necessary to modify or change the goals, as in this case. It is crucial to have the group members set and modify their own objectives, and set their own priorities (Harbert & Ginsberg, 1992).

In this setting, as in the other settings presented in this book, a combination of generic principles of social work practice and specialized knowledge about older persons is essential. Expertise regarding the type of setting in which the social worker is practicing is also required; and social workers must make a connection between the individual, the group, and the organization.

QUESTIONS FOR DISCUSSION: CASE 1

1. What generic principles of social work practice are evident in this case example?
2. How did the agency setting influence the tasks of the group?
3. What factors suggest that older adults are a strong force?
4. What were the roles of the social worker in this case?
5. How can the social worker mediate in this conflict?

CASE EXAMPLE 2:
AN INEFFECTIVE OMBUDSMAN PROGRAM

This second case illustrates the effective use of legislative advocacy as a social work skill.

> The executive director of the state agency on aging is a social worker. As a new appointee to the position, she recognizes a need in the organization for a strong ombudsman program. The staff of this program is responsible for investigating incidents of abuse in nursing homes. During the past 2 years, the problem of such abuse has escalated. The ombudsman program is inadequately funded, and only one full-time paid employee and six volunteers investigate complaints about abuse for the entire state. It is obvious that there is a considerable backlog of complaints awaiting investigation and delays in the imposition of sanctions against facilities or persons responsible for abuse or neglect.
>
> Each year at a legislative hearing of a Joint Committee on Aging, community leaders advocate legislation for older persons in the state. This year a concentrated effort was made by the executive director of the state unit on aging—the social worker—to present testimony by family members on the abuse that their relatives endured in nursing homes. At the end of the day's testimony, it was obvious that the effort by the executive director was successful and the committee would develop new legislation and increase funding for the ombudsman program.

COMMENTS ON CASE EXAMPLE 2

In this case the social worker applies generic principles of macro-level social work practice to gerontological practice. The social worker must do more than be concerned about abuse in nursing homes. The social worker makes an effort to reach those persons who can make changes in the laws on behalf of older people. In this case the social worker planned an advocacy campaign to reach legislators who could make a difference. The effort was successful, and new funding was provided for the program.

QUESTIONS FOR DISCUSSION: CASE EXAMPLE 2

1. What are the tasks of the social worker?
2. What are the potential problems for the social worker?
3. What competing interests must be balanced?

CASE EXAMPLE 3: DIRECTOR OF SOCIAL WORK SERVICES IN A HOSPITAL

The third case illustrates gerontological social work practice in an administrative setting.

A social worker, Ruth Danesh, is the Director of Social Work Services in a local hospital. Her administrative tasks include planning a budget for the department, hiring and firing social work staff, training staff, conducting interdisciplinary case meetings, planning family support groups, planning discharges, interagency collaboration, and community education programs. Ruth Danesh conducts programs such as education programs for families of people with Alzheimer's disease, support groups for spouses, and caregiver groups. Ruth's skills in teamwork are especially useful in this position, because it is necessary in this setting to bring together professionals from medicine, nursing, psychiatry, recreation, speech, physical therapy, and social work to plan goals for the care of patients.

Ruth proposes changes in policies which will be cost-effective and will also protect patients. An example of a policy which needs reexamining is the state's "bed hold" policy. While a patient from a nursing home is being treated in an acute care hospital, the Medicaid system or the patient (privately) pays to hold his or her bed in the nursing home, in some cases for as long as 20 days.

An administrator who is a trained social worker can effectively balance the needs of the client and the needs of the organization. The social work administrator operates from an ethical point of view that values both the client and the organization.

COMMENTS ON CASE EXAMPLE 3

The social worker uses practice skills and gerontological knowledge to develop programs for clients and families, balances the needs of families and the organization, supervises the staff, promotes collaboration among disciplines, and advocates social changes in a system that is not cost-effective and does not always enhance the lives of older persons in its care.

QUESTIONS FOR DISCUSSION: CASE EXAMPLE 3

1. How does being a social worker influence the work of the administrator?
2. What social work skills are needed for effective practice in this case?

3. What knowledge of older adults is necessary for this social work administrator?
4. In what areas is a social work administrator more effective than one trained in other disciplines?
5. How does the agency benefit from hiring a social work administrator?
6. What social work values are evident in this case?

In this chapter we have discussed gerontological social work practice in the political environment. We defined the political environment as an arena for social change that can be accomplished by solving social problems, advocacy, community organizing, program development, and administrative work in organizations. We used case examples to illustrate each of these concepts. We have shown how principles of social work practice can be integrated with knowledge of aging and specialized settings for effective gerontological social work practice.

REFERENCES

Brueggemann, W. G. (1996). *The practice of macro social work.* Chicago, IL: Nelson-Hall.

Burnside, I., & Schmidt, M. G. (1994). *Working with older adults: Group process and techniques.* (3rd ed.) Boston: Jones and Bartlett.

Gelfand, D. (1993). *The aging network: Programs and services* (4th ed.) New York: Springer.

Harbert, A. S., & Ginsberg, L. (1990). *Human services for older adults.* (2nd ed.) Columbia. SC: University of South Carolina Press.

Homan, M. S. (1994). *Promoting community change.* Pacific Grove, CA: Brooks/Cole.

Schwartz, W., & Zalba, S. (1971). *The practice of group work.* New York: Columbia University Press.

Solomon, R. (1992) In M.J. Mellor and R. Solomon (Eds.), *Geriatric social work education* (pp. 112–114). New York: Haworth.

CHAPTER 11

Communication Skills for Gerontological Social Work Practice

I n this chapter we discuss communication skills for gerontological social work practice. Throughout the book, we have emphasized the importance of the *relationship* in social work practice. Social work practice requires the development of a relationship between the client and the professional; social work differs from other professions in that the social worker uses relationship to implement the process. We believe that the key to developing a relationship between social worker and client is effective communication, defined as "the act of transmitting, giving or exchanging information, ...by talk, gestures"(Guralink,1974). Communication with older adults requires specialized knowledge. To communicate effectively with older adult clients, the gerontological social worker must be knowledgeable in the biopsychosocial aspects of aging. We will discuss the biopsychosocial knowledge needed to make a comprehensive assessment of the client's situation. We then explain nonverbal and verbal skills that can be used effectively in gerontological social work practice.

BIOPSYCHOSOCIAL KNOWLEDGE NEEDED FOR COMMUNICATION

MEDICAL KNOWLEDGE

The need for medical knowledge is one reason for the importance of a comprehensive assessment. In the assessment, the social worker gathers information about the client's medical condition and functional status. Clients' medical problems—such as heart disease or cancer—affect their client's ability to communicate. If a client has recently undergone chemotherapy, for instance, its debilitating effects must be considered. Similarily, fatigue and weakness resulting from illnesses are important factors to consider when older adults are interviewed.

"Almost every organ shows some decline in functional or reserve capacity with age" (Hooyman & Kiyak, 1996 p.102). The social worker must be knowledgeable about changes in the cardiovascular, respiratory, gastrointestinal, urinary, and nervous systems, and even changes in the sleep patterns of older adults.

As a result of internal and external stresses older people are vulnerable to mental health problems—in other words, the stresses of old age create a higher risk of psychopathology. Internal stresses may be physiological or psychological. External stresses—such as losses related to roles and functioning—death of a spouse, loss of a job, and so on— are significant factors in an older person's mental health. The primary affective disorder of old age is depression. Alzheimer's disease, alcoholism, and drug abuse can all significantly impact cognitive functioning.

Mental problems such as depression and anxiety are impediments to the process of gathering information from a client and communicating with the client. A depressed client may not provide accurate information, may be unwilling to expend the energy needed to become involved in communication, or may be withdrawn and uncommunicative with the social worker. A person suffering from depression may have low energy or may be fatigued, indecisive or unable to concentrate (American Psychiatric Association, 1994, p. 327). An anxious client can be irritable, irrational, or confused and unable to comprehend the social worker's information.

Polypharmacy is also a problem that can impede the communication process. The interaction of medications can impede clients' physical functioning as well as their psychological functioning. For example, overmedication can cause lethargy, slurred speech, and cognitive deficiencies. Certainly, dementia significantly interferes with intelligence, memory, and learning ability. All dementias have certain problems in common: inability to recall events, impaired comprehension, short attention span, impaired judgment, and poor orientation to time, place, and person (Hooyman & Kiyak, 1996).

SENSORY CHANGES

Obviously, our ability to see, hear, touch, taste, and smell influences our interactions with the social and physical environment. We must be aware of how changes in sensory abilities influence people's relationship to the social environment (Hooyman & Kiyak, 1996). Changes in vision and hearing must be determined in the comprehensive assessment of the client. Such changes include sensory processes, perception, sensation, and sensory discrimination. Problems with vision can affect functioning in activities of daily living. Poor eyesight, glaucoma, and cataracts have a profound effect on people's ability to relate to others. Many older adults report significant changes in their activities of daily living as a result of loss of vision: such as in reading, in driving, and in social activities such as playing cards, cooking, and hobbies (sewing, crafts, movies). Reading documents may be a problem for older adults. The ability to read and comprehend material should, therefore, be determined in the assessment. For example, older adults are asked to sign admission papers when entering a nursing home or retirement home, but the information stated in these documents may not be well understood if a person has sensory or perceptual problems, thus it is incumbent on the social worker to assess the clients' ability to understand the documents that they are asked to sign.

Improvements in the physical environment can improve the functioning of people with visual impairments. Better lighting, large-print books and documents, contrasting color strips, stoves with readable knobs, and large-print labels on prescription bottles and cooking supplies can all help people to maintain their independence. Large-scale architectural and environmental modifications can also help an older person with vision problems to function safely and independently.

Hearing loss can disrupt our understanding of others and our ability to communicate effectively. Tone of voice and use of language are two elements of communication that are significantly affected by impaired hearing. Some researchers have found that hearing problems lead to social isolation and reduced intellectual functioning. Others have found that hearing loss does not significantly affect older people's social functioning—but there is some clinical evidence that older persons with a diagnosis of paranoia are more likely than other elderly people to have hearing problems (Hooyman & Kiyak, 1996).

One of the first signs of hearing loss may be a deterioration in comprehension of speech. An individual with a loss of hearing may deal with it raising the volume of, say, a television or radio, or by becoming isolate Useful techniques for communicating with older persons with hearing los: include the following (Hooyman & Kiyak 1996, p. 124):

- Face an older person directly.
- Sit somewhat close.
- Do not cover your face with your hands while speaking.
- Do not shout.

- Avoid distracting background noises by selecting an appropriate place away from traffic, machines, or people.
- Speak in a lower voice, but not in a monotone.
- Speak slowly and clearly, but without exaggerated speech patterns.
- Repeat key points in different ways.

Sensory changes of normal aging affect a substantial number of older persons. Since these changes, particularly in hearing and vision, affect communication, it is necessary to change the physical environment and alter communication styles in order to reduce their impact.

COGNITIVE FUNCTIONING

Cognitive functioning includes intelligence, learning, and memory. Communication is substantially affected by a person's cognitive functioning. An older person's cognitive functioning should be assessed to determine functional level and to decide which communication techniques should be used with him or her.

Intelligence includes the ability to acquire and comprehend information. Although a social worker is not expected to measure a client's intelligence it is necessary to determine the client's ability to comprehend information. Research findings have indicated that changes in intelligence tests scores are related to problems with physical health. Researchers have observed what seems to be a rapid decline in cognitive functioning within the 5 years preceeding death. This hypothesized phenomenon is known as "terminal drop" (Kleemeier, 1962; White & Cunningham, 1988).

Learning and memory are also cognitive processes. Learning is the process by which new information is put into memory. Memory is the process of retrieving information stored in the brain. Interference with these processes by illness or disease can hinder effective communication.

If the learning process is disrupted an older person will not be able to store information in memory. Also, if new information is not communicated effectively, faulty information will be stored. Thus it it important to realize that the use of words familiar to older persons results in better learning, whereas the use of less familiar words hinders understanding. Some studies have also found that older persons process nonverbal information at a slower rate than younger persons. For example, in a study involving photos of faces, recall was consistently worse among older persons than younger persons (Hooyman & Kiyak, 1996).

Researchers have found age-related differences in memory including recall and recognition (Hooyman & Kiyak, 1996). "Interference theory" appears to hold the most promise for explaining observed problems of older persons with retrieval. It suggests that poor retrieval is due to distraction during the learning stage. This theory needs to be considered with regard to communication techniques that are used with older persons.

CULTURAL DIFFERENCES

Ethnogerontology refers to the causes, processes, and consequences of race, national origin, and culture on the aging of individuals and populations. It is essential for gerontological social work practitioners to understand the client's culture and to consider the communication patterns of older persons in that culture. Clients' behaviors are often a result of ethnic background, and communication styles vary from culture to culture. For example, in Asian cultures eye contact is considered disrespectful. To take another example, many languages have formal and informal words or styles of communication and professionals should use a formal style when communicating with older persons. Older African Americans (among others) tend to consider the use of first names disrespectful.

In cross-cultural interactions, the social worker must learn to react appropriately to situations that are a result of a client's values. Cultural competence in communication implies that the worker is respectful of the ethnic differences of the client's system and accommodates herself or himself to the context within which the client functions. For instance, many cultures use nonverbal communication to a much greater extent than verbal communication (Kirst-Ashman & Hull, 1993). In Asian American cultures, facial expressions and gestures convey more than words. Native American communication is also considered to be more nonverbal than verbal. This is a quiet culture; Native Americans do not self-disclose readily, nor do they share information which may be shameful (Kirst-Ashman & Hull, 1993). Some nonverbal gestures may be confusing. For example, a Japanese man may nod his head simply to show that he is following the conversation, and this can be misinterpreted as a sign of understanding or agreement. With Native Americans it is easy to mistake respect for passivity, because Native Americans frequently do not respond—as a sign of respect for the professional. In nonverbal communication, as noted above, the worker must also remember that eye contact can be a problem for some ethnic groups.

In their discussion of communication techniques, Kirst-Ashman and Hull (1993) suggest the use of both open-ended and close-ended questions with various cultures because such questions are almost universally acceptable. They state that reflection of feelings works with many cultures, but not with all cultures. They indicate that rephrasing is an acceptable technique in most cultures, and they suggest summarizing from time to time. But they say confrontation must be used carefully with certain racial groups.

GENDER AND AGE-RELATED DIFFERENCES

The communication patterns of women and men are different. Gender- and age-related differences are obvious in the use of language and the expression of familiarity.

Empathy tends to be an effective communicating skill with women, since women tend to be more empathetic than men. Research findings suggest that females tend to score higher on measures of empathy than males (Haynes & Holmes, 1994). These gender-based differences in empathy are probably best explained by differences in the socialization of males and females (Haynes & Holmes, 1994). Also, empathy is a useful technique because it fits well with feminist principles of counseling. Feminist intervention emphasizes that clients need encouragement to free themselves from traditional gender roles—and they need to focus on their strengths rather than their pathologies. Women need to be encouraged to develop relationships in which they are not dependent, and to develop their identity on the basis of their own strengths, achievements, and individuality. Stressful life events such as separation, divorce, or death of a spouse are especially difficult for women. Frequently women find it difficult to establish autonomy. The stereotyped feminine role encourages women to listen, to care, and to understand but prohibits them from expressing what they need, want, think, and feel. An older women is likely to have been socialized with these attitudes, and it is essential for the gerontological social worker to be sensitive to the effects of gender and to use effective communication techniques.

NONVERBAL SKILLS

Messages conveyed by nonverbal behavior can contradict spoken words. When contradictory messages are sent, it is often the nonverbal message that is received. Nonverbal messages may indicate that a social worker has no interest in a client, does not understand the client, or is uncomfortable with the client. The social worker must therefore pay attention to nonverbal messages such as confusion, anxiety, or lack of interest.

Three important aspects of nonverbal communication are:

- *Personal space.* A client may be uncomfortable if a social worker invades his or her personal space. In some cultures (such as the Vietnamese) it is considered disrespectful for a male to be alone in a closed room with an adult female. It may thus be important for the worker to avoid such a situation (Kirst-Ashman & Hull, 1993).
- *Facial expressions.* Facial expressions indicate much about the client's attentiveness and feelings. Sadness, happiness, anxiety, concern, and confusion are easily detected in facial expressions. Facial expressions are very important in Hispanic communication patterns (Kirst-Ashman & Hull,1993).
- *Body language.* The client's attitude may also be reflected in body language. Is the client facing the social worker? Is the client sitting or standing rigidly? Is the client fidgeting? Is the client twisting or turning?

VERBAL SKILLS AND TECHNIQUES

Essentially, we communicate verbally. Therefore, as already mentioned, a comprehensive assessment of the older person's ability to communicate or to be involved in the communication process with the social worker is essential. The next step is to use selective techniques when communicating with older persons. These include the following.

EMPATHY

Empathy is the ability to see and feel the world as another person sees and feels it. It includes an ability to understand and appreciate another's point of view, in fact, it requires taking on someone else's point of view—"If I were in that person's circumstances, I might think, feel, or do exactly as he or she thinks, feels or does." The social worker must make an accurate assessment of the client's perceptions and the significance of those perceptions to the client. In social work practice, we often use the maxim "Start where the client is." However, we must first know where the client is, and then be able to communicate to the client that we understand. Empathy is essential in a relationship. It is important for a client to be liked and supported, but even more important to be understood. Being understood is the beginning of being valued. It leads to trust and to developing a relationship. Being empathetic is an important ingredient of the helping process, and learning to convey that empathy is essential. Empathy is a skill. The social worker must learn to be intentionally and consistently empathetic. Some tools for learning to be empathetic are the following:

- *Believe that it matters.* It is essential for the social worker to appreciate the importance of empathy in order to practice empathetic responses consistentlywith clients. This is initially a conscious effort but later becomes a habit.
- *Focus on the other person.* Although there are many things that compete for a worker's attention, it is most important to give the client full attention. It is important to listen to the client and not to move on to a new subject until the client is ready. It is necessary to focus one's mind on the client—not the next appointment or other work that must be done.
- *Focus on the other person's feelings.* Although a social worker may have never been in the situation that a particular client is in, the social worker can connect with the client's feeling. For example, we can all connect with the sadness of losing a loved one. We can all connect with being frightened, lonely, and anxious. It is important to connect with the feeling rather than the situation.
- *Be open to change yourself.* When you really try to understand another person, your own perceptions may be challenged. Be prepared to learn from others.
- *Ask for feedback.* In expressing empathy, it is helpful to use feedback and to use a "stem" such as , "You feel____ " to show that you understand the ideas or perceptions being expressed.
- *Allow the client to correct you.* Allowing a client to correct you indicates that you have interpreted a message accurately.
- *Describe the causes of feelings.* Try to describe possible causes of the client's feelings. For example, "You are angry because you feel abandoned by your friends."
- *Respond frequently.* Allow the client to tell the story, and express your empathy frequently.
- *Respond briefly.* When rephrasing a client's story, be brief.
- *Use body language to express empathy*—facial expressions, touch, and use of personal space. Smile, touch when appropriate, and sit close to the client if possible. Face the client and look directly at him or her.

EXERCISES FOR EXPRESSING EMPATHY

For each client statement, write a response using the format, " You feel___
because___."

1. My brother went off and left me to take care of our mother last year. I
   do everything for her and take very good care of her. When my brother
   visits once or twice a year, my mom treats him as if he has been the
   one taking care of her each day. She even talks about changing her
   will and leaving him the house.

   Response: You feel _____

   _____

   because _____

   _____ .

2. I've worked hard all my life and always made do with what I had. I
   don't need a social worker to tell me how to live my life now that I'm
   old. It's my business—not yours—if I don't want to see a doctor about
   the pains in my legs. I've managed to live this long without your help,
   and I can do just fine.

   Response: You feel _____

   _____

   because _____

   _____ .

3. My daughter says that I need to go into a nursing home. I won't go. I'd
   rather die here in my own home. I am getting along just fine.

   Response: You feel _____

   _____

   because _____

   _____ .

4. "Don't tell me you understand how I feel. A young person like you can't understand how it is to be old. You are too young to know how awful it is to be old. When you are old, nobody listens to you."

Response: You feel _____

_____

because _____

_____ .

5. "Don't you tell me you understand how I feel. You're White, so you can't know how a Black person feels. You come here with your good education and your good job and you tell me I've got to try harder. What do you know about trying? You've had everything handed to you from the day you were born.

Response: You feel _____

_____

because _____

_____ .

FORMULATING QUESTIONS

In interviewing clients for a comprehensive assessment of their situation, it is essential to learn to formulate questions. Gathering information is an essential skill in the assessment process. Being able to uncover information from the client, the family, and other systems depends on asking the right questions. A social worker must know when to ask "open" questions and when to ask "closed" questions. Open questions are often more difficult to phrase than closed questions. Following are important types of questions.

- *Closed questions.* Closed questions focus on facts, elicit specific information, define a topic, and restrict a client's response. Direct questions ask *who, what, when, where, how many,* and *how long* and focus on a specific piece of information. Example: "How many times have you been in the hospital this year?" Closed questions provide specific information and are good for data collection. They are the quickest way to find out specific information, especially when time is short or a client is very talkative. But they have the disadvantage that the client may not volunteer other information—information that may be very pertinent. Another disadvantage is that a series of direct questions may be seen as an interrogation.

- *Yes-no questions.* These are very specific questions that ask only for a yes or no answer. "Did you attend the meeting?" This kind of question is useful in confrontations, but it provides very limited information, and clients may feel that they are being interrogated.

- *Choice questions.* The client must select from a limited number of alternatives, for example, "Would you prefer to see the doctor on Monday or Wednesday?" This type of question gives the client some sense of control.

- *Leading questions.* A leading question suggests what the answer should be; for example, "You didn't drink this morning, did you?" This type of question makes assumptions and thus provides an opportunity for inaccurate responses.

- *"Why" questions.* This type of question causes the clients to justify their behavior. For example: "Why did you leave her unattended?"

- *Open questions.* An open question invites an expansive answer and leaves the client free to express what he or she feels is important. It elicits more information and helps create a more relaxed atmosphere. It allows the social worker to share responsibility and control with the client. For example: "Could you tell me a little more about that?" A disadvantage of open questions is that a talkative client can ramble and the worker may lose control of the interview.

- *Statement questions.* A statement question is one that calls for elaboration on the part of the client. For example: "Tell me how you felt when it had happened." This type of question allows the client to offer additional information, and to explore feelings and motivations.

EXERCISES FOR OPEN-ENDED RESPONSES

Write an open-ended question in response to each statement by a client.

1. *Client:* I don't want to give up my apartment. I've always been independent until I fell and broke my hip. I know I can't clean the way I used to, but I can manage here.

   Worker: _____

2. *Client:* When mother moved in with us, we knew it wouldn't be easy, but we never expected so much trouble. I just don't know how to handle her irrational behavior any more.

Worker: _____

3. *Client:* My children want me to move to a senior apartment complex near them but I have been living in this neighborhood for 40 years. I don't want to leave my friends and my church.

Worker: _____

FEEDBACK

Feedback provides information about some aspect of another person's behavior and its impact. Feedback gives a client insight into his or her own behavior. It allows the social worker to express feelings, and it may result in behavioral change. When giving feedback it is necessary to do so as soon as possible after the behavior has occurred. Do not filter feedback through a third party. Be direct, and describe specific behaviors. For example, "When you raise your voice, it makes me think you are angry."

HUMOR

Humor involves offering lighthearted comments—comments that are intended to be funny or to bring out the comical side of a conversation or situation. Humor can help to reduce tension in a relationship and can help the client to see the worker as a person.

UNIVERSALIZATION

In this technique, the worker makes comments to indicate that a behavior or situation is not unusual but is in fact relatively common or normal. Universalization thus helps the client to feel more "normal." It may help to clarify a client's issues and can elicit statements about the client's feelings. Using the statement, " Many people___ " may help to relieve a client's anxiety about a situation or behavior.

REFRAMING

Reframing is restating a client's statement in a way that puts the idea into a new perspective. The worker should suggest positive ways of looking at situations which the client sees as negative. Reframing changes the client's cognitive set, and this allows for more freedom of thoughts and ideas. For example: "It sounds as if your mother is being difficult. I wonder, though, if she is not just trying to express her independence." When reframing, paraphrase or summarize the client's statement before going on to state an alternative point of view—and state the reframed version tentatively. Be concise in reframing. Do not use psychological or social work jargon or theories.

"I" MESSAGES AND "YOU" MESSAGES

When a worker responds to the misbehavior or mistakes of a client with judgmental statements, the client's feelings of self-worth can be affected. A *judgmental statement* is one that criticizes the person rather than—as is appropriate—the behavior. In other words, it is important to focus on the behavior, not the person. "You" messages are negative messages about a person. By contrast, "I" messages are constructive statements aimed at changing the behavior, not the person. Examples of "you" messages are: "Why can't *you* be neater?" "*You* are drunk." "*You* are lazy." To repeat, messages that concentrate on *you* are judgments. Messages that concentrate on *I* are reactions. "I" messages tell people how their behavior affects the people around them. An "I" message focuses on a particular behavior, not on worthiness of a client. For example, in contrast to the "you" message "You are always late for your appointments," an "I" message would be: "I find it difficult to have my schedule delayed by late appointments." In contrast to the "you" message "You are being nasty," an "I" message would be, "I find it hard to work with someone who is in such a bad mood."

EXERCISES ON "YOU" MESSAGES AND "I" MESSAGES

Write an "I" statement to replace each judgmental "you" statement.
1. Mrs. Carter is an 85-year-old woman with no mental deterioration. She is very frail, having broken her arm twice in the past 3 years. She has just been hospitalized for a broken hip. She lives alone in the home she has owned for 50 years. She refuses to leave her home or to have anyone live with her.

"You" message: "You are being very stubborn. You know that you can't take care of yourself."

"I" message: _____

2. Cosmo T. is living in a nursing home and is very angry. He argues with the nurses, refuses to bathe, is hostile to his daughter, and will not leave his room.

"You" message: "You are a very difficult person. You are making life miserable for the staff and your family."

"I" message _____

CONFRONTATION

Confrontation can be an effective communication skill. Social workers have to confront their clients frequently about tasks undone, conflicting statements, and perceptions that conflict with reality. Confrontative statements should be factual, should not place blame, and should be for the good of the other person in the relationship. Confrontation is often seen as negative and hostile, but in communicating with clients it can be used in a positive sense to change behavior or thinking. It is a technique which allows the worker to challenge the client's narrow or distorted view of reality to allow for change. It is necessary for growth.

EXERCISES ON CONFRONTATION

1. An aged client insists that his injuries—multiple fractures in various stages of healing and bruises in the shape of a belt buckle—were caused by falling down a flight of stairs. The doctor has advised you that none of the injuries is consistent with a fall. You confront the client. _____

_____ .

2. A client states that she can live alone quite adequately. She is 85 years old and was released from the hospital last week. She is unable to get out of bed alone, cannot stand long enough to prepare meals, and cannot leave the house unaccompanied. She has multiple chronic illnesses and lives in a trailer home in a rural isolated area. She has no family in the area. You confront her: _____

_____ .

SILENCE

It is often helpful to be silent for a period of time. Silence allows the worker and client to have some time to think. It can be used as a way to modify inappropriate behavior. It can allow a client to express emotions. It makes a client feel that his or her feelings and opinions are respected. It gives the client time for introspection and is especially important with clients who take some time to respond.

In this chapter we have presented the specialized knowledge needed to communicate with older persons. It must include medical information and knowledge of sensory changes and cognitive functioning. Cultural sensitivity and gender sensitivity are essential for effective communication with all age groups. However, age-related differences in cohorts must be recognized in communicating with older adults. We have discussed the importance of being aware of nonverbal cues—body language, personal space, and facial expressions—in order to understand clients' behavior. Finally, specific verbal techniques were presented with illustrations and exercises. These techniques have been used successfully by social workers we have trained.

REFERENCES

American Psychiatric Association (1994). *Diagnostic and statistical manual of mental disorders,* (4th ed.).Washington, DC: Author.

Cavanaugh, J.C. (1996). *Adult development and aging,* (3rd Ed.) Pacific Grove, CA: Brooks/Cole.

Guralink, D. (1974). *Webster's new world dictionary.* (2nd College ed.) New York: Collins/World.

Haynes, K. S., & Holmes , K. A.(1994). *Invitation to social work.* New York: Longman.

Hooyman, N., & Kiyak, Y. (1996). *Social gerontology* (4th ed.) Boston: Allyn and Bacon.

Kirst-Ashman, K., & Hull, G. (1993). *Understanding generalist practice.* Chicago: Nelson-Hall.

Kleemeier, R.W. (1961, August). Intellectual change in the senium, or death and the IQ. Presidential address. New York: American Psychological Association.

White, N., & Cunningham, W.R. (1988). Is terminal drop pervasive or specific? *Journal of Gerontology, 43,* 141–144.

Epilogue:
Implications and Conclusions

The approach presented in this book demonstrates the application of functional principles to the practice of social work in gerontological settings. These principles underscore the importance of the agency's function in defining the roles of the social worker and client in the helping process. The functional orientation also emphasizes the worker-client relationship as a key to movement in the process. We have attempted to demonstrate that functionalism is not an archaic approach but in fact embraces many of the principles of modern psychoanalytic theory in its focus on such factors as setting limits and the relationship as critical to the client's progress. In each setting of social work, a combination of general and specialized knowledge is required. General knowledge of the biological, psychological and social aspects of aging is critical to comprehensive assessment and to the identification of clients' needs. However, each setting also requires specialized expertise, and we have addressed the subtleties of practice in arenas as diverse as hospitals, law offices, religious organizations, and the corporation.

Social work is unique in its concern with both the individual and the social group as targets of helpful intervention. The functional approach integrates these two concerns in a conceptual framework that links clients' movement with organizational change. The idea is that the social worker cannot properly attend to the needs of clients without simultaneously intervening in areas that have an impact on the individual's personal situation, such as the family, a social agency, or an institutional setting. Since the role of the worker is linked to the agency's purpose, that purpose must reflect

146

the needs of clients, or else it will be obsolete and counterproductive.

The thoughts presented in these pages are particularly timely because of the continued growth in bureaucratic organizational structures. Organizations are being replaced by mega-organizations, and social workers and other health practitioners are being constrained by precepts of managed care. These principles of managed care are governed by a focus as much on economy as on the quality of service delivery. This places added pressure on social workers to actively mediate between clients' needs and the purposes of the organizations that serve them. In addition, the increased centrality of the "human resource" function in organizations—with a growing awareness of the relationship between employees' morale, their productivity, and the quality of the product—is further evidence of the connection between individual and group functioning.

Functionalism is the denominator that links social work professionals in various fields of practice. It does not preclude the need for specialization. It does not even necessarily run counter to developments in psychoanalytic theory. But it does offer a unique framework that defines social work as distinct from other mental health professions.

The approach presented in these pages demonstrates the applicability of functional concepts to gerontological social work practice in a variety of fields. The methodology has implications for research, education, and social policy.

Many will argue the relative merit of other orientations in contrast to functional concepts. We would suggest that an enlightened emphasis on integrating helping strategies—rather than debunking any particular orientation—should be the standard for development of theory for the profession. Glaser and Strauss (1967) formulated a research methodology for building social theory that relies on the technique of constant comparison to test the accuracy of ideas, including concepts of practice. Functionalism may have greater relevance in certain areas of practice than in other areas, and comparative analysis would distinguish more accurately between the generic and the specific aspects of social work in different fields. The functional approach seems to be extremely relevant to work with the current generation of older people because of their own priorities for growth and change, and because of their reliance on institutional resources.

We hope that this book has offered an opportunity for students and professionals to struggle with concepts of practice and to clarify their understanding of their work with older people. We feel that the importance of this book derives especially from our case examples. We would like the reader to come away not so much with our point of view as with a point of view.

Finally, we are proud of our social work heritage and we hope that we have imparted a sense of our pride. Social work, above all other mental health professions, offers a foundation for helping people *and* their institutions. We have the theory and technology to affect policy and to translate causes into functions. We have broken much new ground since Ruth Smalley wrote her classic work. It is incumbent on us to remember our covenant with our clients and our society: "to release human power in individuals" and "to release social power" for the creation of the "kinds of society" which make self-realization possible (Smalley, 1967, p. 1).

REFERENCES

Glaser, B., & Strauss, A. (1967). *The discovery of grounded theory.* Chicago: Aldine.

Smalley, R. (1967). *Theory for social work practice.* New York: Columbia University Press.

Glossary

Agency's function The purpose, goal, or overriding mission of an institution.

Diagnosis An understanding of the client's need for service.

Function in professional role The focus of a worker's activities. This represents the task which defines the scope of the worker-client interaction.

Functional social work An approach to social work practice that emphasizes "function in professional role" (see above) and relationship to the client's growth. The functional approach differs from the traditional diagnostic approach in its emphasis on the client's health rather than on pathology—and in the centrality of clients to the definition of their own understanding of their needs.

Integrative model of gerontological social work A framework for gerontological social work practice that combines generalist principles with specialized knowledge of older people and particular fields of practice (e.g., legal, medical, and religious).

Relationship The connection or alliance between the worker and the client, which develops by means of communication or interaction. In the functional approach, the relationship is guided by the social work task, which derives from the agency's function.

Social work method A relationship process in which the worker helps the individual or group to use or modify the service being provided.

Social work modalities The particular contexts or systems in which relationships develop (e.g., case, group, community, administrative). The casework method, for example, is the social work method or relationship process employed in the delivery of a service to an individual client within the casework modality.

Appendix: Multidisciplinary Screening Instrument

Instructions: Indicate presence, absence, and/or need for further referral after conducting a simple, minimally structured face-to-face interview.

	<u>Yes</u>	<u>No</u>	<u>Referral</u>
Appearance			
Is the client neatly and appropriately dressed?	❑	❑	❑
Is the client's clothing clean?	❑	❑	❑
Is client's hair neatly combed?	❑	❑	❑
Is the client clean?	❑	❑	❑
Does the client make eye contact?	❑	❑	❑
When he/she interacts with the interviewer, does the client make involuntary movements?	❑	❑	❑
Affect			
Are the client's mood and reactions appropriate to the interview situation?	❑	❑	❑
Intellect			
Are there any indicators that the client's abstract thinking is impaired?	❑	❑	❑
Memory			
Assess short-term memory with questions like:			
Did you have breakfast today?	❑	❑	❑
What did you eat?	❑	❑	❑
Assess long-term memory with questions like:			
Do you remember your birth date?	❑	❑	❑

Judgment

Does the client understand that a problem exists?	❑	❑	❑
Does the client propose a solution?	❑	❑	❑
Does the client's suggestion demonstrate a sound grasp of the current situation?	❑	❑	❑
Is the client able to recognize that one of the solutions must be implemented?	❑	❑	❑

Orientation

Is the client able to identify the date, familiar people, and himself or herself?	❑	❑	❑

Level of Independence

Is the person able to live independently?	❑	❑	❑

Physical Limitations

Is the individual's ability to move hampered in any way?	❑	❑	❑
Is the client's hand-grip sufficient for ordinary day-to-day activities?	❑	❑	❑
Does the client have impaired vision?	❑	❑	❑
Does the client have any apparent hearing loss?	❑	❑	❑

Index

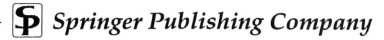
Ṩ *Springer Publishing Company*

Gerontology, Second Edition
Perspectives and Issues
Kenneth Ferraro, PhD

Designed as a text for graduate and advanced graduate studies, this volume is a comprehensive overview of the state of knowledge in aging. Dr. Ferraro emphasizes the multidisciplinary nature of gerontology and the need for an overarching theoretical paradigm, or "a gerontological imagination," to unite the field. The book is designed to articulate systemically the most current aspects of aging including: demographics, biology, psychology, and sociology, as well as medicine, nursing, social work, and health education.

The new edition has been updated to include information on caregiving, social policy debates, and the economic status of the older population and to continue the on-going dialogue of how the field of gerontology is growing. It is an ideal primary text for courses in gerontology or a supplemental text for discipline-based courses in related fields.

Contents: **Introduction to Gerontology.** The Gerontological Imagination • Demography of Aging in the United States • **Salient Perspectives in Gerontology.** Biology of Aging • Neurogerontology: The Aging Nervous System • Psychology of Aging: Stability and Change in Intelligence and Personality • Sociology of Aging: The Micro/Macro Link • Cross-Cultural Comparisons of Aging • **Aging in the Institutional Context.** Reciprocity Between Family Generations • Work and Retirement • Religion and Aging • Long-Term Care • Family Caregiving: A Focus for Aging Research and Invention • **Contemporary Issues in an Aging Society.** Ethnogerontology: Social Aging in National, Racial and Cultural Groups • Economic Status of Older Adults in the United States: Diversity, Women's Disadvantage, and Policy Implications • Promoting Healthy Aging • Elder Abuse and Neglect • Aging and Crime • Death, Dying and the Will to Live • Is Gerontology a Multidisciplinary or Interdisciplinary Field of Study? Evidence from Scholarly Affiliations and Educational Programming

1997   432pp   0-8261-6661-X   hardcover

536 Broadway, New York, NY 10012-3955 • (212) 431-4370 • Fax (212) 941-7842

P Springer Publishing Company

Elderly Men
Special Problems and Professional Challenges

Jordan I. Kosberg, PhD and **Lenard W. Kaye,** DSW

This book provides an interdisciplinary overview of common and unique features of elderly men and how they age. The editors examine cultural, psychological, physical, and economic factors which affect the quality of life for older men. They clearly illustrate the diversity within this population, highlighting ethnicity, religion, and important socio-demographic variables. The volume presents elderly men as a minority in need of critical examination to understand more fully this "forgotten population." The text's practical application will appeal to both students and practitioners in the fields of social work and gerontology.

Contents:
Theorizing About Older Men, *J.S. Applegate* • A Demographic Overview of Elderly Men, *W.P. Magnum* • Older Men and the Workplace: Breaking New Ground, *D.L. Wagner* • Elderly Men of the Inner-City, *J.K. Ekert and L. G. Repaci* • Men in Retirement Communities, *B.D. Dunlop, M.B. Rothman, and C. Ramnbali* • Elderly Men in Prisons, *W.A. Formby, and C. Abel* • Rural Older Men: A Neglected Elderly Population, *J.A. Krout, Jan McCulloch, and V.R. Kivett* • Gay Men in Later Life, *G.S. Getzel* • The Transition to Retirement, *A. Monk* •The Physical Health of Older Men: The Significance of the Social and Physical Environment, *W.A. Satarino* • Recognizing and Treating Alcohol Abuse and Alcohol Dependence in Elderly Men, *K.J. Farkas and L.A. Kola* • Mental Disorders of Elderly Men, *J.L. McIntosh, J.L. Pearson, and B. Lebowitz* • The Victimization of Elderly Men, *J.I. Kosberg and S.L. Bowie* • Informal Caregiving by Older Men, *L.W. Kaye* • Community Programs and Services, *S.S. Tobin* • Support Groups for Older Men: Building on Strengths and Facilitating Relationships, *T.H. Koff* • The Status of Older Men: Current Perspectives and Future Projections, *J.I. Kosberg and L.W. Kaye*

Springer Series: Focus on Men
1997   360pp   0-8261-9670-5   *hardcover*

536 Broadway, New York, NY 10012-3955 • (212) 431-4370 • Fax (212) 941-7842

SP *Springer Publishing Company*

Matching People With Services in Long-Term Care

Zev Harel, PhD and **Ruth E. Dunkle,** PhD

Incorporating perspectives from both social and health sciences, the editors and contributors of this book describe the special needs of people requiring long-term care, and make recommendations for improving delivery of long-term care services, both in institutions and in the growing home care arena.

Part I offers a critical review of the characteristics and needs of vulnerable adults and the current patterns of long-term care programs and services. Part II analyzes a range of long-term care services, including informal caregivers, home-based and community-based services, services offered in institutional settings, and those used by special populations. This book is useful for health and social service professionals who work with the aged, as well as academics and students in long-term care, sociology, public health, nursing, health administration, and policymakers.

Contents:

Severe Vulnerability and Long-Term Care, *Z. Harel & L. S. Noelker* • People Using Long-Term Care Services, *M. Smith & C. Longino* • Ethnic/Racial Diversity in Long-Term Care, *J. Skinner* • Complex Long-Term Care System, *T. Fairchild, J. Knebl, and D. Burgos* • Special Community Settings, *R. Rubenstein* • Veterans and Long-Term Care Services, *J. Damron-Rodriguez and M. Cantrell* • Long-Term Care Services: Process and Outcome, *R. Dunkle & M. Stone* • Caregivers: Resources and Services, *D. Montcalm* • Community and Home-Based Programs and Services, *Z. Harel & B. Harel* • Institutional Settings: Programs and Services, *C. Kart and R. Dunkle* • Serving Cognitively Impaired Adults and Aged, *K. Smyth* • Serving Sensory Impaired Elderly in Long-Term Care, *D. Ripich* • Protective Services and Long-Term Care, *G. Anetzberger*

1995   304pp   0-8261-8950-4   hardcover

536 Broadway, New York, NY 10012-3955 • (212) 431-4370 • Fax (212) 941-7842

ℙ *Springer Publishing Company*

The Aging Network
Programs and Services, 4th Edition
Donald E. Gelfand, PhD

This fully updated edition of a highly successful text serves as a "roadmap" to care providers for the elderly. It focuses on the present status of older Americans, income maintenance programs, Medicare and Medicaid, and provides readers with details on major programs in aging ranging from information and assistance efforts to crime prevention programs.

Contents:

I: **The American Elderly.** The Older American • Legislative Bases for Programs and Services

II: **Income Maintenance Programs.** Age, Employment, and Income Maintenance, *J. Berman and D.E. Gelfand* • Illness, Medical Care, and Income Maintenance, *J. Berman and D.E. Gelfand*

III: **Programs for the Aged.** Information and Assistance • Health and Mental Health • Transportation • Crime and Legal Assistance Programs • Employment, Volunteer, and Educational Programs • Nutrition Programs

IV: **Services for the Aged.** Multipurpose Senior Centers • Housing • In-Home Services • Adult Daycare • Long-Term Care Residences • The Future of Aging Programs and Services

V: **Appendices.** National Nonprofit Resource Groups in Aging • The Older Americans Act of 1992

1993   440pp   0-8261-3056-9   softcover

536 Broadway, New York, NY 10012-3955 • (212) 431-4370 • Fax (212) 941-7842